Gospel Of Mark In English And Mandarin...

American Bible Society

書音福可馬

THE GOSPEL OF MARK

IN

ENGLISH AND MANDARIN.

PUBLISHED BY THE

AMERICAN BIBLE SOCIETY.

SHANGHAI:

AMERICAN PRESBYTERIAN MISSION PRESS.

1884.

馬傳福音書

THE GOSPEL ACCORDING TO MARK.

CHAPTER I.

THE beginning of the gospel of Jesus Christ, the Son of God ;

2 As it is written in the prophets, Behold, I send my messenger before thy face, which shall prepare thy way before thee.

3 The voice of one crying in the wilderness, Prepare ye the way of the Lord, make his paths straight.

4 John did baptize in the wilderness, and preach the baptism of repentance for the remission of sins.

5 And there went out unto him all the land of Judea, and they of Jerusalem, and were all baptized of him in the river of Jordan, confessing their sins.

6 And John was clothed with camel's hair, and with a girdle of a skin about his loins ; and he did eat locusts and wild honey ;

7 And preached, saying, There cometh one mightier than I after me, the latchet of whose shoes I am not worthy to stoop down and unloose.

8 I indeed have baptized you with water : but he shall baptize you with the Holy Ghost.

9 And it came to pass in those days, that Jesus came from Nazareth of Galilee, and was baptized of John in Jordan.

10 And straightway coming up out of the water, he saw the heavens opened, and the Spirit like a dove descending upon him :

11 And there came a voice from heaven, *saying*, Thou art my beloved Son, in whom I am well pleased.

第一章

神的兒子耶穌基督福音的起頭先知書上記著說我要差遣我的使者在你面前、預備你的道路、在

曠野有人聲喊叫說預備　主的道修直了他的路照這話有約翰在曠野施洗傳悔改的洗禮使罪得

赦猶太全地、和耶路撒冷的人、出去到約翰那裏都承認自己的罪惡在約但河受他的洗約翰穿駱駝

毛的衣服腰繫皮帶、吃的是蝗蟲野蜜他傳道說有比我能力更大的在我以後來、我就是屈身爲他解

鞋帶、也是不配的、我是用水與你們施洗他將用　聖靈與你們施洗○那時候耶穌從加利利的拏撒

勒來、在約但河裏受了約翰的洗他從水裏上來、就看見天開了、　聖靈彷彿鴿子降在他頭上

12 And immediately the Spirit driveth him into the wilderness.

13 And he was there in the wilderness forty days tempted of Satan; and was with the wild beasts; and the angels ministered unto him.

14 Now after that John was put in prison, Jesus came into Galilee, preaching the gospel of the kingdom of God,

15 And saying, The time is fulfilled and the kingdom of God is at hand: repent ye, and believe the gospel.

16 Now as he walked by the sea of Galilee, he saw Simon and Andrew his brother casting a net into the sea: for they were fishers.

17 And Jesus said unto them, Come ye after me, and I will make you to become fishers of men.

18 And straightway they forsook their nets, and followed him.

19 And when he had gone a little further thence, he saw James the *son* of Zebedee, and John his brother, who also were in the ship mending their nets.

20 And straightway he called them: and they left their father Zebedee in the ship with the hired servants, and went after him.

21 And they went into Capernaum; and straightway on the sabbath day he entered into the synagogue, and taught.

22 And they were astonished at his doctrine: for he taught them as one that had authority, and not as the scribes.

23 And there was in their synagogue a man with an unclean spirit; and he cried out,

24 Saying, Let *us* alone; what have we to do with thee, thou Jesus of Nazareth? art thou come to destroy us? I know thee who thou art, the Holy One of God.

25 And Jesus rebuked him, saying, Hold thy peace, and come out of him.

又有聲音從天上來說、你是我的愛子、我所喜悅的。 聖靈就叫他往曠野去。他在那裏住了四十日受撒但的試探和野獸同住、並且有天使服事他。○約翰下監以後耶穌到了加利利傳 神國的福音說日期到了、 神的國近了、你們應當悔改信福音。○耶穌在加利利的海邊行走、看見西門和他兄弟安得烈、在海裏撒網、他們本是打魚的人耶穌對他們說、來跟從我、我要叫你們得人如得魚一樣他們就丟下網、跟從了耶穌從那裏稍往前走、又看見西庇太的兒子雅各和雅各的兄弟約翰在船上補網。耶穌叫他們來、他們就別了父親西庇太、留他和雇工人在船上跟從了耶穌。○到了迦百農耶穌就在安息日進了會堂教訓人衆人聽他的教訓、都甚詫異因為他教訓人正如有權柄的人不同那讀書人在會堂裏有一個被邪鬼附著的人、喊叫說拏撒勒的耶穌我們和你甚麼相干、你來滅我們麼、我曉得你是誰、就是 神的聖者。耶穌責備他說不要作聲從這人身上出來罷。

26 And when the unclean spirit had torn him, and cried with a loud voice, he came out of him.

27 And they were all amazed, insomuch that they questioned among themselves, saying, What thing is this? what new doctrine *is* this? for with authority commandeth he even the unclean spirits, and they do obey him.

28 And immediately his fame spread abroad throughout all the region round about Galilee.

29 And forthwith, when they were come out of the synagogue, they entered into the house of Simon and Andrew, with James and John.

30 But Simon's wife's mother lay sick of a fever; and anon they tell him of her.

31 And he came and took her by the hand, and lifted her up; and immediately the fever left her, and she ministered unto them.

32 And at even, when the sun did set, they brought unto him all that were diseased, and them that were possessed with devils.

33 And all the city was gathered together at the door.

34 And he healed many that were sick of divers diseases, and cast out many devils; and suffered not the devils to speak, because they knew him.

35 And in the morning, rising up a great while before day, he went out, and departed into a solitary place, and there prayed.

36 And Simon and they that were with him followed after him.

37 And when they had found him, they said unto him, All *men* seek for thee.

38 And he said unto them, Let us go into the next towns, that I may preach there also: for therefore came I forth.

39 And he preached in their synagogues throughout all Galilee, and cast out devils.

邪鬼叫那人抽了一陣瘋、大聲喊着就出來了衆人驚訝彼此問說這是怎樣的事、這是甚麼新道理呢、因爲他用權柄吩咐

邪鬼、鬼也聽從他。耶穌的聲名就傳遍加利利的四方了。○衆人出了會堂耶穌和雅各約翰進了西門安得烈的家裏西門

的岳母、患熱病躺臥、有人來告訴耶穌耶穌前去拉那婦人的手扶他起來、熱病立刻退了、婦人就服事他們。到晚上日落的

時候、有人帶着一切患病的、被鬼附的、到耶穌這裏來合城的人、都聚集在門前、耶穌醫好許多患各樣病的人又趕出許多

鬼不許鬼說話、因爲鬼認識他。○天未亮的時候耶穌早早起來、到曠野去、在那裏禱告西門和他的同伴追了耶穌來遇見

他、就說、衆人尋找你、耶穌說、我們往附近的鄉村去、我也要在那裏講道因我是特爲這事來的。於是在加利利各處會堂講

道趕鬼。

40 And there came a leper to him, beseeching him, and kneeling down to him, and saying unto him, If thou wilt, thou canst make me clean.

41 And Jesus, moved with compassion, put forth *his* hand, and touched him, and saith unto him, I will ; be thou clean.

42 And as soon as he had spoken, immediately the leprosy departed from him, and he was cleansed.

43 And he straitly charged him, and forthwith sent him away ;

44 And saith unto him, See thou say nothing to any man.: but go thy way, shew thyself to the priest, and offer for thy cleansing those things which Moses commanded, for a testimony unto them.

45 But he went out, and began to publish *it* much, and to blaze abroad the matter, insomuch that Jesus could no more openly enter into the city, but was without in desert places : and they came to him from every quarter.

CHAPTER II.

AND again he entered into Capernaum after *some* days; and it was noised that he was in the house.

2 And straightway many were gathered together, insomuch that there was no room to receive *them*, no, not so much as about the door: and he preached the word unto them.

3 And they come unto him, bringing one sick of the palsy, which was borne of four.

4 And when they could not come nigh unto him for the press, they uncovered the roof where he was: and when they had broken *it* up, they let down the bed wherein the sick of the palsy lay.

5 When Jesus saw their faith, he said unto the sick of the palsy, Son, thy sins be forgiven thee.

○有一個長瘋的人來求他跪下說你若肯必能叫我乾淨了耶穌發了憐憫的心伸手摸他說我肯你乾淨了罷說著瘋病立刻離了他的身人就乾淨了耶穌叫他去切切的囑付他說你要謹愼不可告訴人要去叫祭司察看你的身體因爲你乾淨了獻上摩西所吩咐的禮物在衆人面前作憑據那人出去竟說許多的話傳揚這件事叫耶穌以後不得明顯進城只好在野外居住人從四方都就了他來。

第二章

過了幾日耶穌又進迦百農人聽見他在屋裏就有許多人聚集連門外都沒有空地了耶穌對他們講道有人帶一個患癱瘋病的來見耶穌用四個人擡著因爲人多不得進前就拆那房頂旣拆通了將患癱瘋的人連牀都縋下來。耶穌見他們這樣信他就對患癱瘋的人說小子你的罪赦了。

6 But there were certain of the scribes sitting there, and reasoning in their hearts,

7 Why doth this *man* thus speak blasphemies? who can forgive sins but God only?

8 And immediately, when Jesus perceived in his spirit that they so reasoned within themselves, he said unto them, Why reason ye these things in your hearts?

9 Whether is it easier to say to the sick of the palsy, *Thy* sins be forgiven thee; or to say, Arise, and take up thy bed, and walk?

10 But that ye may know that the Son of man hath power on earth to forgive sins, (he saith to the sick of the palsy,)

11 I say unto thee, Arise, and take up thy bed, and go thy way into thine house.

12 And immediately he arose, took up the bed, and went forth before them all; insomuch that they were all amazed, and glorified God, saying, We never saw it on this fashion.

13 And he went forth again by the sea side; and all the multitude resorted unto him, and he taught them.

14 And as he passed by, he saw Levi the *son* of Alpheus sitting at the receipt of custom, and said unto him, Follow me. And he arose and followed him.

15 And it came to pass, that, as Jesus sat at meat in his house, many publicans and sinners sat also together with Jesus and his disciples; for there were many, and they followed him.

16 And when the scribes and Pharisees saw him eat with publicans and sinners, they said unto his disciples, How is it that he eateth and drinketh with publicans and sinners?

17 When Jesus heard *it*, he saith unto them, They that are whole have no need of the physician, but they that are sick: I came not to call the righteous, but sinners to repentance.

有幾個讀書人坐在那裏心裏議論這個人、怎麼說這樣僭妄的話呢、除了　神以外、誰能赦罪、耶穌心裏曉得他們這樣議論、就說、你們爲甚麼心裏這樣議論對患癱瘋的人說你的罪赦了、或說起來拏你的牀行走那一樣容易呢、現在要叫你們曉得人子在世上有赦罪的權柄就對患癱瘋的人說我吩咐你起來拏你的牀囘家去罷那人立刻起來、在衆人面前拏著牀出去了、衆人驚異歸榮耀與　神、說、我們從來沒有見過這樣的事、○耶穌又出去到海邊、有許多人來見他、耶穌便教訓他們、再往前走看見亞勒腓的兒子利未坐在稅關上就對他說、你跟從我來、利未就起來、跟從他去了、○耶穌在利未家裏坐席、有許多稅吏和罪人來、與耶穌並耶穌的門徒一同坐席、因爲這樣的人跟隨耶穌的不少讀書人和法利賽人見耶穌與稅吏並罪人同席喫飯、就對他的門徒說、他爲甚麼與稅吏並罪人一同喫喝呢、耶穌聽見就對他們說健壯的人用不著醫生、患病的人纔用得著我來、不是要叫義人悔改、是要叫罪人悔改。

18 And the disciples of John and
of the Pharisees used to fast: and they
come and say unto him, Why do the
disciples of John and of the Pharisees
fast, but thy disciples fast not?

19 And Jesus said unto them, Can
the children of the bridechamber fast,
while the bridegroom is with them?
as long as they have the bridegroom
with them, they cannot fast.

20 But the days will come, when
the bridegroom shall be taken away
from them, and then shall they fast
in those days.

21 No man also seweth a piece of
new cloth on an old garment; else the
new piece that filled it up taketh away
from the old, and the rent is made
worse.

22 And no man putteth new wine
into old bottles; else the new wine
doth burst the bottles, and the wine is
spilled, and the bottles will be marred:
but new wine must be put into new
bottles.

23 And it came to pass, that he
went through the corn fields on the
sabbath day; and his disciples began,
as they went, to pluck the ears
of corn.

24 And the Pharisees said unto
him, Behold, why do they on the
sabbath day that which is not lawful?

25 And he said unto them, Have
ye never read what David did, when
he had need, and was a hungered,
he, and they that were with him?

26 How he went into the house of
God in the days of Abiathar the high
priest, and did eat the shewbread,
which is not lawful to eat but for the
priests, and gave also to them which
were with him?

27 And he said unto them, The
sabbath was made for man, and not
man for the sabbath:

28 Therefore the Son of man is
Lord also of the sabbath.

○約翰的門徒、和法利賽人的門徒、常常禁食、有人來對耶穌說、約翰的門徒、和法利賽人的門徒禁食、你的門徒不禁食、是爲甚麼呢、耶穌囘答說、新郎和慶賀新郎的人同在的時候、慶賀的人怎能禁食呢、有新郎同在、他們不能禁食、將來新郎離開他們去了、那時候他們必要禁食、沒有孲新布補舊衣服的、恐怕所補的新布反帶壞了舊衣服、破的更大了、也沒有將新酒盛在舊皮袋裏的、恐怕新酒裂了皮袋、酒漏出來、連皮袋也壞了、新酒只當盛在新皮袋裏○當安息日、耶穌從麥田經過、他門徒行路的時候、摘了麥穗、法利賽人對耶穌說、他們在安息日做不當做的事、是爲甚麼呢、耶穌囘答說、經上記著、大闢和跟隨他的人乏用飢餓的時候所做的事、你們沒有讀過麼、大闢在亞庇亞塔做祭司長的時候、進了 神的殿、喫了陳設的餅、並且給跟隨他的人喫、這餅除了祭司以外、人都不當喫。又對他們說、安息日是爲人設立的、人不是爲安息日設立的、所以人子也是安息日的主。

CHAPTER III.

AND he entered again into the synagogue; and there was a man there which had a withered hand.

2 And they watched him, whether he would heal him on the sabbath day; that they might accuse him.

3 And he saith unto the man which had the withered hand, Stand forth.

4 And he saith unto them, Is it lawful to do good on the sabbath days, or to do evil? to save life, or to kill? But they held their peace.

5 And when he had looked round about on them with anger, being grieved for the hardness of their hearts, he saith unto the man, Stretch forth thine hand. And he stretched *it* out: and his hand was restored whole as the other.

6 And the Pharisees went forth, and straightway took counsel with the Herodians against him, how they might destroy him.

7 But Jesus withdrew himself with his disciples to the sea: and a great multitude from Galilee followed him, and from Judea,

8 And from Jerusalem, and from Idumea, and *from* beyond Jordan; and they about Tyre and Sidon, a great multitude, when they had heard what great things he did, came unto him.

9 And he speak to his disciples, that a small ship should wait on him because of the multitude, lest they should throng him.

10 For he had healed many; insomuch that they pressed upon him for to touch him, as many as had plagues.

11 And unclean spirits, when they saw him, fell down before him, and cried, saying, Thou art the Son of God.

12 And he straitly charged them that they should not make him known.

13 And he goeth up into a mountain, and calleth *unto him* whom he would: and they came unto him.

第三章

一耶穌又進了會堂、在那裏有一個枯乾一隻手的人、二衆人窺探耶穌、在安息日醫他不、意思要控告耶穌。三耶穌對那枯乾手的人說你起來、站在中間就問衆人說在安息日、做善事、做惡事、救生命害生命、那是應當的呢、他們都不作聲耶穌怒目周圍看衆人、憂愁他們心太硬、就對那人說伸出你的手來、那人將手一伸、手就好了、像那隻手一樣。六法利賽人出去、和希律一黨的人大家商議怎樣可以殺害耶穌。○耶穌同門徒離了那地方、往海邊去有許多人從加利利猶太耶路撒冷以土買約但河外來跟隨他、還有推羅西頓許多的人聽見他所做的事、也就到他來。九耶穌因爲人多就吩咐門徒預備小船、免得受他們的擁擠。耶穌醫好許多人、所以凡有病的、都進到他面前要摸他。耶鬼一見他、就俯伏在他面前、喊叫說你是 神的兒子。耶穌切切的囑附他們、不要告訴人。○耶穌上了山、隨意叫人來、人就來了。

14 And he ordained twelve, that they should be with him, and that he might send them forth to preach,

15 And to have power to heal sicknesses, and to cast out devils:

16 And Simon he surnamed Peter;

17 And James the *son* of Zebedee, and John the brother of James; and he surnamed them Boanerges, which is, The sons of thunder:

18 And Andrew, and Philip, and Bartholomew, and Matthew, and Thomas, and James the *son* of Alpheus, and Thaddeus, and Simon the Canaanite,

19 And Judas Iscariot, which also betrayed him: and they went into a house.

20 And the multitude cometh together again, so that they could not so much as eat bread.

21 And when his friends heard *of it*, they went out to lay hold on him: for they said, He is beside himself.

22 ¶ And the scribes which came down from Jerusalem said, He hath Beelzebub, and by the prince of the devils casteth he out devils.

23 And he called them *unto him*, and said unto them in parables, How can Satan cast out Satan?

24 And if a kingdom be divided against itself, that kingdom cannot stand.

25 And if a house be divided against itself, that house cannot stand.

26 And if Satan rise up against himself, and be divided, he cannot stand, but hath an end.

27 No man can enter into a strong man's house, and spoil his goods, except he will first bind the strong man; and then he will spoil his house.

28 Verily I say unto you, All sins shall be forgiven unto the sons of men, and blasphemies wherewith soever they shall blaspheme:

便設立十二個人、要他們常和自己在一處、又要差遣他們去傳道並賜他們醫病趕鬼的權柄、十二人有西門耶穌又賜名

與他叫彼得還有西庇太的兒子雅各和雅各的兄弟約翰這兩個人又賜名叫半尼其意思就是雷子又有安得烈腓力巴

多羅買馬太多馬亞勒腓的兒子雅各和達太並稱銳的西門、還有賣耶穌的以色加略猶大。○他們進了屋衆人又聚集、

以致他們連喫飯也不能。耶穌的親屬聽見就出來、要拉住他說他是癲狂了有讀書人從耶路撒冷下來說、他是被別西卜

附著靠鬼王趕鬼的耶穌叫他們來用比喻對他們說撒但怎能逐出撒但呢、又說國若自相分爭國必站立不住家若自相

分爭家必站立不住撒但若自相攻打分爭他也站立不住必要滅亡沒有人能進勇士的家裏搶掠他的家具、必先捆住那

勇士後緣可以搶掠他的家財。我實在告訴你們、世人無論犯甚麼罪、無論說甚麼毀謗的話、都可以赦免他、

29 But he that shall blaspheme against the Holy Ghost hath never forgiveness, but is in danger of eternal damnation.

30 Because they said, He hath an unclean spirit.

31 ¶ There came then his brethren and his mother, and, standing without, sent unto him, calling him.

32 And the multitude sat about him, and they said unto him, Behold, thy mother and thy brethren without seek for thee.

33 And he answered them, saying, Who is my mother, or my brethren?

34 And he looked round about on them which sat about him, and said, Behold my mother and my brethren!

35 For whosoever shall do the will of God, the same is my brother, and my sister, and mother.

CHAPTER IV.

AND he began again to teach by the sea side: and there was gathered unto him a great multitude, so that he entered into a ship, and sat in the sea; and the whole multitude was by the sea on the land.

2 And he taught them many things by parables, and said unto them in his doctrine,

3 Hearken; Behold, there went out a sower to sow:

4 And it came to pass, as he sowed, some fell by the way side, and the fowls of the air came and devoured it up.

5 And some fell on stony ground, where it had not much earth; and immediately it sprang up, because it had no depth of earth:

6 But when the sun was up, it was scorched; and because it had no root, it withered away.

7 And some fell among thorns, and the thorns grew up, and choked it, and it yielded no fruit.

惟有毀謗聖靈的人、永不得赦免、必要受永遠的刑罰耶穌說這話、因爲人說他是被邪鬼附著的。○當下耶穌的母親和他弟兄來了、站在外面打發人去叫他、衆人在耶穌周圍坐著、有人告訴他說你的母親和你的弟兄在外面尋找你、耶穌囘答說誰是我的母親誰是我的弟兄就四面觀看周圍坐著的人說你們看我的母親我的弟兄凡遵行 神的旨意的人就是我的弟兄我的姐妹我的母親了。

第四章

耶穌又在海邊教訓人、有許多人聚集在他面前他就上船坐下、船在海裏那許多人都沿著海邊站在岸上。耶穌用比喻多多的教訓他們、教訓的時候、對他們說、你們聽著、有撒種的人、出去撒種撒的時候、有落在道旁的、空中的雀鳥來喫盡了。有落在土薄有石頭的地上的、土旣淺薄發苗最快、日頭出來一曬、因爲沒有根就枯乾了。有落在荆棘裏的、荆棘長起來、將苗遮蔽住了、就不能結實。

8 And other fell on good ground, and did yield fruit that sprang up and increased, and brought forth, some thirty, and some sixty, and some a hundred.

9 And he said unto them, He that hath ears to hear, let him hear.

10 And when he was alone, they that were about him with the twelve asked of him the parable.

11 And he said unto them, Unto you it is given to know the mystery of the kingdom of God: but unto them that are without, all *these* things are done in parables:

12 That seeing they may see, and not perceive; and hearing they may hear, and not understand; lest at any time they should be converted, and *their* sins should be forgiven them.

13 And he said unto them, Know ye not this parable? and how then will ye know all parables?

14 ¶ The sower soweth the word.

15 And these are they by the way side, where the word is sown; but when they have heard, Satan cometh immediately, and taketh away the word that was sown in their hearts.

16 And these are they likewise which are sown on stony ground; who, when they have heard the word, immediately receive it with gladness;

17 And have no root in themselves, and so endure but for a time: afterward, when affliction or persecution ariseth for the word's sake, immediately they are offended.

18 And these are they which are sown among thorns; such as hear the word,

19 And the cares of this world, and the deceitfulness of riches, and the lusts of other things entering in, choke the word, and it becometh unfruitful.

20 And these are they which are sown on good ground; such as hear the word, and receive *it*, and bring forth fruit, some thirtyfold, some sixty, and some a hundred.

有落在好土裏的、就發生起來長大了、結實有三十倍的、有六十倍的、有一百倍的。又說凡有耳可聽的、都應當聽。衆人散後、

跟從耶穌的人、和十二門徒、問這比喩是甚麽意思耶穌囘答說、神國的奧祕只賜與你們知道若是外人凡事就用比喩

敎訓他們、叫他們看見也不曉得聽見也不明白恐怕他們囘心轉意他們的罪就得赦免又說這比喩你們不懂怎能懂得

各樣比喩呢。撒種的就是傳道的人。撒在道旁的就是說人聽了所傳的道、撒但就來、將所撒在他們心裏的道奪了去撒在

有石頭的地上的就是說人聽道的時候便歡喜領受只因他心裏沒有根也不過是暫時的、及至爲道遇患難受迫害、就厭

棄了撒在荆棘裏的、就是說人聽道又有世上的思慮貨財的迷惑並各樣的情欲、進來遮蔽了道就不能結實撒在好地上

的、就是說人聽道便領受並且結實有三十倍的有六十倍的有一百倍的。

21 ¶ And he said unto them, Is a candle brought to be put under a bushel, or under a bed? and not to be set on a candlestick?

22 For there is nothing hid, which shall not be manifested; neither was any thing kept secret, but that it should come abroad.

23 If any man have ears to hear, let him hear.

24 And he said unto them, Take heed what ye hear. With what measure ye mete, it shall be measured to you; and unto you that hear shall more be given.

25 For he that hath, to him shall be given; and he that hath not, from him shall be taken even that which he hath.

26 ¶ And he said, So is the kingdom of God, as if a man should cast seed into the ground;

27 And should sleep, and rise night and day, and the seed should spring and grow up, he knoweth not how.

28 For the earth bringeth forth fruit of herself; first the blade, then the ear, after that the full corn in the ear.

29 But when the fruit is brought forth, immediately he putteth in the sickle, because the harvest is come.

30 ¶ And he said, Whereunto shall we liken the kingdom of God? or with what comparison shall we compare it?

31 It is like a grain of mustard seed, which, when it is sown in the earth, is less than all the seeds that be in the earth:

32 But when it is sown, it groweth up, and becometh greater than all herbs, and shooteth out great branches; so that the fowls of the air may lodge under the shadow of it.

33 And with many such parables spake he the word unto them, as they were able to hear it.

○耶穌又說、人拏燈來豈是放在斗底下、牀底下、不是放在燈臺上麼、因爲嚴密的事、沒有不現出來的、隱藏的事、沒有不露出來的。

凡有耳可聽的、都應當聽、又說、你們聽道要留心、你們用甚麼量器量給人、人也用甚麼量器量給你們、並且要加倍

賜給你們這聽道的人、因爲有的人還要加給他、沒有的人連他所有的也要奪過來。○又說、　神的國、如同人將種撒在地

上、日裏醒著、夜裏睡著、那種發芽長大、這人也不曉得如何、這人因爲地土本是能生五穀的、先發苗、後長穗、再後穗上結滿

了穀實、旣是熟了、就用鐮刀去割、因爲收成的時候到了。○又說、　神的國是像甚麼、可用甚麼比喻來比呢、比如一粒芥菜

種、種在地裏的時候、是地上百樣種裏最小的、種了之後、就生出來、比各樣菜都大、又長了大枝、空中的鳥可以住在他的陰

涼裏、又用許多這樣的比喻、對他們講道、都照著他們所能聽的。

34 But without a parable spake he not unto them : and when they were alone, he expounded all things to his disciples.

35 And the same day, when the even was come, he saith unto them, Let us pass over unto the other side.

36 And when they had sent away the multitude, they took him even as he was in the ship. And there were also with him other [little] ships.

37 And there arose a great storm of wind, and the waves beat into the ship, so that it was now full.

38 And he was in the hinder part of the ship, asleep on a pillow: and they awake him, and say unto him, Master, carest thou not that we perish ?

39 And he arose, and rebuked the wind, and said unto the sea, Peace, be still. And the wind ceased, and there was a great calm.

40 And he said unto them, Why are ye so fearful ? how is it that ye have no faith ?

41 And they feared exceedingly, and said one to another, What manner of man is this, that even the wind and the sea obey him?

CHAPTER V.

AND they came over unto the other side of the sea, into the country of the Gadarenes.

2 And when he was come out of the ship, immediately there met him out of the tombs a man with an unclean spirit,

3 Who had *his* dwelling among the tombs; and no man could bind him, no, not with chains :

4 Because that he had been often bound with fetters and chains, and the chains had been plucked asunder by him, and the fetters broken in pieces: neither could any *man* tame him.

5 And always, night and day, he was in the mountains, and in the tombs, crying, and cutting himself with stones.

若不是比喻、就不對他們說、到沒有人的時候、將這些比喻、都講解給門徒聽、當日晚上、對門徒說、我們渡到那邊岸上去、耶穌仍坐在船上、門徒遣散了眾人、就開船去了、又有別的船同行、忽然狂風大起、波浪翻騰、打進船裏、水將要滿了船、耶穌在船尾上枕著枕頭睡覺、門徒叫醒了他、對他說夫子、我們要死了、你不顧麼、耶穌起來、指斥風對海說住了罷、風就止住、大大平靜了、耶穌說你們為甚麼這樣懼怕、怎麼不信呢、他們都驚恐得很、彼此說這是怎樣的人、連風和海、都聽從他了。

第五章

他們來到海那邊、加大拉的地方、耶穌下了船、就有被邪鬼附著的人、從墳墓裏出來、遇見他、那人素常伕在墳墓裏、人就是用鐵鍊捆他、也捆不住、因為人屢次用脚鐐和鐵鍊捆他、鐵鍊被他掙斷、脚鐐被他扭壞、總沒有人能制伏他、晝夜常在山中、在墳墓裏喊叫、又用石頭打傷自己、

6 But when he saw Jesus afar off, he ran and worshipped him,

7 And cried with a loud voice, and said, What have I to do with thee, Jesus, *thou* Son of the most high God? I adjure thee by God, that thou torment me not.

8 (For he said unto him, Come out of the man, *thou* unclean spirit.)

9 And he asked him, What *is* thy name? And he answered, saying, My name *is* Legion: for we are many.

10 And he besought him much that he would not send them away out of the country.

11 Now there was there nigh unto the mountains a great herd of swine feeding.

12 And all the devils besought him, saying, Send us into the swine, that we may enter into them.

13 And forthwith Jesus gave them leave. And the unclean spirits went out, and entered into the swine; and the herd ran violently down a steep place into the sea, (they were about two thousand,) and were choked in the sea.

14 And they that fed the swine fled, and told *it* in the city, and in the country. And they went out to see what it was that was done.

15 And they come to Jesus, and see him that was possessed with the devil, and had the legion, sitting, and clothed, and in his right mind; and they were afraid.

16 And they that saw *it* told them how it befell to him that was possessed with the devil, and *also* concerning the swine.

17 And they began to pray him to depart out of their coasts.

18 And when he was come into the ship, he that had been possessed with the devil prayed him that he might be with him.

遠遠的看見耶穌就跑上前來拜他、大聲呼叫說、至上　神的兒子耶穌、我與你有甚麼關涉我奉　神的名求你不要叫我受苦、因爲耶穌曾吩咐他說邪鬼、離開這個人罷耶穌問他你叫甚麼名囘答說我名叫羣因爲我們多的緣故就懇求耶穌不要趕逐他們離開這地方、在那裏山邊上、有一大羣豬喫食衆鬼求耶穌說容我們往豬羣裏附著豬去、耶穌許了他們、邪鬼就出離人身、進入豬羣、那羣豬闖下山坡、投在海裏淹死了、豬數約有二千放豬的跑去告訴城裏鄉下的人衆人都出來、要看所做的是甚麼事、到了耶穌那裏見那從前被鬼所附的人坐著、穿上衣服、心裏明白過來、他們就懼怕了、那看見耶穌趕鬼的、就將被鬼附的人所遇的、和那一羣豬的事、都告訴他們衆人便求耶穌離開他們的境界、耶穌上船的時候、那從前被鬼附的人、懇求耶穌準他和耶穌在一處。

19 Howbeit Jesus suffered him not, but saith unto him, Go home to thy friends, and tell them how great things the Lord hath done for thee, and hath had compassion on thee.

20 And he departed, and began to publish in Decapolis how great things Jesus had done for him : and all *men* did marvel.

21 And when Jesus was passed over again by ship unto the other side, much people gathered unto him; and he was nigh unto the sea.

22 And, behold, there cometh one of the rulers of the synagogue, Jairus by name ; and when he saw him, he fell at his feet,

23 And besought him greatly, saying, My little daughter lieth at the point of death : *I pray thee*, come and lay thy hands on her, that she may be healed ; and she shall live.

24 And *Jesus* went with him ; and much people followed him, and thronged him.

25 And a certain woman, which had an issue of blood twelve years,

26 And had suffered many things of many physicians, and had spent all that she had, and was nothing bettered, but rather grew worse,

27 When she had heard of Jesus, came in the press behind, and touched his garment.

28 For she said, If I may touch but his clothes, I shall be whole.

29 And straightway the fountain of her blood was dried up ; and she felt in *her* body that she was healed of that plague.

30 And Jesus, immediately knowing in himself that virtue had gone out of him, turned him about in the press, and said, Who touched my clothes?

31 And his disciples said unto him, Thou seest the multitude thronging thee, and sayest thou, Who touched me?

耶穌不准對他說你問家到你親眷那裏去將　主怎樣待你怎樣憐憫你、告訴他們那人去了在低加波利就訴說耶穌向

他所行的事衆人都詫異〇耶穌上了船又渡到那邊岸上去有許多人到他那裏聚集他正在海邊上有一個管會堂的人

來了名叫睚魯見了耶穌就俯伏在他脚前切切的求他說我的小女兒快死了請你來按手在他身上醫治他他必活了耶

穌同他去有許多人跟隨擁擠著他有一個婦人患了十二年血漏的病在許多醫生手裏受了許多的苦費盡所有的家財就

毫不見好病勢反利害了這婦人聽見耶穌的名聲就從後頭雜在衆人中間摸耶穌的衣服意思說我只摸耶穌的衣服、就

必痊愈他的血漏立刻止住覺得身上的病已經好了耶穌心裏覺得有能力從自己出來就在衆人中間轉過來說誰摸我

的衣服門徒說你看衆人擁擠你怎麽倒問誰摸我呢。

32 And he looked round about to see her that had done this thing.

33 But the woman fearing and trembling, knowing what was done in her, came and fell down before him, and told him all the truth.

34 And he said unto her, Daughter, thy faith hath made thee whole; go in peace, and be whole of thy plague.

35 While he yet spake, there came from the ruler of the synagogue's *house certain* which said, Thy daughter is dead; why troublest thou the Master any further?

36 As soon as Jesus heard the word that was spoken, he saith unto the ruler of the synagogue, Be not afraid, only believe.

37 And he suffered no man to follow him, save Peter, and James, and John the brother of James.

38 And he cometh to the house of the ruler of the synagogue, and seeth the tumult, and them that wept and wailed greatly.

39 And when he was come in, he saith unto them, Why make ye this ado, and weep? the damsel is not dead, but sleepeth.

40 And they laughed him to scorn. But when he had put them all out, he taketh the father and the mother of the damsel, and them that were with him, and entereth in where the damsel was lying.

41 And he took the damsel by the hand, and said unto her, Talitha cumi; which is, being interpreted, Damsel, (I say unto thee,) arise.

42 And straightway the damsel arose, and walked; for she was of *the age* of twelve years. And they were astonished with a great astonishment.

43 And he charged them straitly that no man should know it; and commanded that something should be given her to eat.

耶穌周圍觀看要見做這事的人。婦人曉得自己身上痊愈就恐懼戰兢俯伏在耶穌面前將實情全告訴耶穌。耶穌說女兒

你的信救了你了平平安安的囘去你的病已痊愈了○還說話的時候有人從管會堂的家裏來說你的女兒死了爲甚麼

還勞動先生耶穌聽見所告訴的話就對管會堂的人說你不要怕只要信於是帶著彼得和雅各的兄弟約翰同行不

許別人跟隨到了管會堂的家裏看見衆人忙亂就跳痛哭進到裏面就對他們說爲甚麼忙亂痛哭呢這女孩兒不是死是

睡覺呢衆人都笑他耶穌叫衆人出去帶了女孩兒的父母和跟隨的人進了女孩兒躺著的地方就拉女孩兒的手對他說

大利大古米繙出來就是說女兒阿我吩咐你起來那女孩兒立刻起來行走他年方十二歲衆人驚異得很耶穌切切的囑

付他們不可叫人曉得這事就吩咐拏東西給女兒喫。

CHAPTER VI.

AND he went out from thence, and came into his own country; and his disciples follow him.

2 And when the sabbath day was come, he began to teach in the synagogue: and many hearing *him* were astonished, saying, From whence hath this *man* these things? and what wisdom *is* this which is given unto him, that even such mighty works are wrought by his hands?

3 Is not this the carpenter, the son of Mary, the brother of James, and Joses, and of Juda, and Simon? and are not his sisters here with us? And they were offended at him.

4 But Jesus said unto them, A prophet is not without honour, but in his own country, and among his own kin, and in his own house.

5 And he could there do no mighty work, save that he laid his hands upon a few sick folk, and healed *them*.

6 And he marvelled because of their unbelief. And he went round about the villages, teaching.

7 ¶ And he called *unto him* the twelve, and began to send them forth by two and two; and gave them power over unclean spirits;

8 And commanded them that they should take nothing for *their* journey, save a staff only; no scrip, no bread, no money in *their* purse:

9 But *be* shod with sandals; and not put on two coats.

10 And he said unto them, In what place soever ye enter into a house, there abide till ye depart from that place.

11 And whosoever shall not receive you, nor hear you, when ye depart thence, shake off the dust under your feet for a testimony against them. Verily I say unto you, It shall be more tolerable for Sodom and Gomorrah in the day of judgment, than for that city.

第六章

耶穌離了那地方來到自己家鄉門徒跟隨他。到了安息日在會堂裏教訓人、衆人聽見便詫異說這人如何能這樣呢、他所裏受的是何等聰明、竟有這樣異能從他手裏出來呢、他不是木匠麼、不是馬利亞的兒子麼、與雅各約西猶大西門不是弟兄麼、他的姐妹不是在我們這裏麼、因此就厭棄他了。耶穌對他們說、大凡先知除了家鄉親戚本族以外、沒有不被人尊敬的。耶穌在那裏不得行甚麼奇事只按手在幾個病人身上醫好他們。又詫異他們不信、就往四面村子上教訓人去了○耶穌叫了十二個門徒來、差遣他們兩個兩個的出去、賜與他們趕逐邪鬼的權柄吩咐他們不要帶路費只帶拐杖不要帶袋、不要帶糧食、腰帶裏不要帶錢只要穿鞋不要穿兩套衣服、又說無論到那裏進了人的家、就住在那裏直到你們去的時候。凡不接待你們的、不聽從你們的、離那裏的時候就抖下你們脚上的塵土對他們作見證我實在告訴你們、到了審判的日子、所多馬蛾摩拉的刑罰比那地方的刑罰還容易受呢。

12 And they went out, and preached that men should repent.

13 And they cast out many devils,
and anointed with oil many that were
sick, and healed *them*.

14 And king Herod heard *of him*;
(for his name was spread abroad;) and
he said, That John the Baptist was
risen from the dead, and therefore
mighty works do shew forth themselves
in him.

15 Others said, That it is Elias.
And others said, That it is a prophet,
or as one of the prophets.

16 But when Herod heard *thereof*,
he said, It is John, whom I beheaded:
he is risen from the dead.

17 For Herod himself had sent
forth and laid hold upon John, and
bound him in prison for Herodias'
sake, his brother Philip's wife; for he
had married her.

18 For John had said unto Herod,
It is not lawful for thee to have thy
brother's wife.

19 Therefore Herodias had a quar-
rel against him, and would have killed
him; but she could not:

20 For Herod feared John, knowing that he was a just man and a
holy, and observed him; and when he
heard him, he did many things, and
heard him gladly.

21 And when a convenient day
was come, that Herod on his birthday
made a supper to his lords, high cap-
tains, and chief *estates* of Galilee;

22 And when the daughter of the
said Herodias came in, and danced,
and pleased Herod and them that sat
with him, the king said unto the
damsel, Ask of me whatsoever thou
wilt, and I will give *it* thee.

23 And he sware unto her, Whatsoever thou shalt ask of me, I will give
it thee, unto the half of my kingdom.

24 And she went forth, and said unto
her mother, What shall I ask? And

門徒出去傳道、勸人悔改、又逐出許多的鬼、用油抹了許多病人醫好他們○耶穌的聲名傳揚出來、希律王聽見便說、這是施洗的約翰從死裏復活、所以能行這些奇事。別人說、是以利亞、還有人說是先知、或是像古時的一個先知。希律聽見就說、這是我所斬的約翰從死裏復活了。先是希律差人拏住約翰鎖在監裏、因爲他兄弟腓力的妻子希羅底的緣故、希律曾娶了他爲妻、約翰對希律說、娶兄弟的妻子、是不合理的。從此希羅底恨約翰、要殺他、郤是不能、因爲希律知道約翰是義人、是聖人、敬畏他、保護他、聽他的話多照著行、並且歡喜聽他的敎訓。一日恰巧是希律的生日、希律擺設筵席、請了許多的大人千夫長、並加利利的尊貴人、希羅底的女兒進來跳舞、希律和同席的人都歡喜、王對女子說、你無論要甚麼、可向我求、我必賜給你。又對他起誓說、凡你向我所求的、就是我國的一半、我必賜給你。女子就出去、對他母親說、我當求甚麼、同答說當求施洗約翰的頭。

she said, The head of John the Baptist.

25 And she came in straightway with haste unto the king, and asked, saying, I will that thou give me by and by in a charger the head of John the Baptist.

26 And the king was exceeding sorry; *yet* for his oath's sake, and for their sakes which sat with him, he would not reject her.

27 And immediately the king sent an executioner, and commanded his head to be brought: and he went and beheaded him in the prison,

28 And brought his head in a charger, and gave it to the damsel; and the damsel gave it to her mother.

29 And when his disciples heard *of it*, they came and took up his corpse, and laid it in a tomb.

30 And the apostles gathered themselves together unto Jesus, and told him all things, both what they had done, and what they had taught.

31 And he said unto them, Come ye yourselves apart into a desert place, and rest a while: for there were many coming and going, and they had no leisure so much as to eat.

32 And they departed into a desert place by ship privately.

33 And the people saw them departing, and many knew him, and ran afoot thither out of all cities, and outwent them, and came together unto him.

34 And Jesus, when he came out, saw much people, and was moved with compassion toward them, because they were as sheep not having a shepherd: and he began to teach them many things.

35 And when the day was now far spent, his disciples came unto him, and said, This is a desert place, and now the time *is* far passed:

36 Send them away, that they may go into the country round about, and into the villages, and buy themselves bread: for they have nothing to eat.

女子急忙進來見王、求他說、請你立刻將施洗約翰的頭、放在盤子裏賜給我、王甚憂愁、無奈已經起誓、並且同席的人都在那裏就不肯推郤、立刻吩咐劊子手去將約翰的頭拿來、那人就去、在監裏斬了約翰、將頭放在盤子裏拿來給女子、女子交給他母親。約翰的門徒聽見就來領屍、葬在墳墓裏○衆使徒聚集來見耶穌、將所做的事、所傳的道、全告訴他、耶穌說你們暗暗的到曠野來、歇息片時、因爲往來的人多、他們連喫飯也沒有工夫。就暗暗的坐船、到野地去了。○衆人看見他們去有許多認得耶穌的、從各城裏步行跑到那裏、比他們先到了、一齊來見耶穌。○耶穌出來、看見衆人、憐憫他們、因爲他們如同羊、沒有牧養的人一般、就將許多的道理敎訓他們、天將晚的時候、門徒來對他說、這是野地、天將晚了、請逼散衆人、叫他們往四面鄕村去買餅、因爲他們沒有食物。

37 He answered and said unto them, Give ye them to eat. And they say unto him, Shall we go and buy two hundred pennyworth of bread, and give them to eat?

38 He saith unto them, How many loaves have ye? go and see. And when they knew, they say, Five, and two fishes.

39 And he commanded them to make all sit down by companies upon the green grass.

40 And they sat down in ranks, by hundreds, and by fifties.

41 And when he had taken the five loaves and the two fishes, he looked up to heaven, and blessed, and brake the loaves, and gave *them* to his disciples to set before them; and the two fishes divided he among them all.

42 And they did all eat, and were filled.

43 And they took up twelve baskets full of the fragments, and of the fishes.

44 And they that did eat of the loaves were about five thousand men.

45 And straightway he constrained his disciples to get into the ship, and to go to the other side before unto Bethsaida, while he sent away the people.

46 And when he had sent them away, he departed into a mountain to pray.

47 And when even was come, the ship was in the midst of the sea, and he alone on the land.

48 And he saw them toiling in rowing; for the wind was contrary unto them: and about the fourth watch of the night he cometh unto them, walking upon the sea, and would have passed by them.

49 But when they saw him walking upon the sea, they supposed it had been a spirit, and cried out:

50 For they all saw him, and were troubled. And immediately he talked with them, and saith unto them, Be of good cheer: it is I; be not afraid.

耶穌囘答說你們給他們喫罷門徒說要我們買二十兩銀子的餅、給他們喫麼、耶穌說你們有多少餅、可去看看、旣看見了、就說有五個餅、兩尾魚。耶穌吩咐他們、叫衆人一排一排的坐在青草地上、衆人就坐下、有一百在一處的、有五十在一處的。耶穌拏著五個餅、兩尾魚望著天、祝謝了、擘開餅、遞給門徒、叫擺在衆人面前、又將兩尾魚分給他們、衆人都喫飽了。收拾碎餅膡魚裝滿了十二筐子、喫餅的人、約有五千。○耶穌催門徒上船、先渡到那邊百賽大去、等自己遣散衆人、耶穌遣散衆人以後、往山上去禱告、天已晚了、船在海中、他獨自一人在岸上、看見門徒因風不順、搖船甚苦、夜裏約有四更時分、耶穌在海面上行走、到門徒這裏來、彷彿要過去的樣子、門徒看見耶穌在海面上行走、以爲是怪物、就喊叫起來、因爲他們看見他、都驚慌了。耶穌連忙對他們說、你們放心、是我、不要懼怕。

51 And he went up unto them into the ship; and the wind ceased: and they were sore amazed in themselves beyond measure, and wondered.

52 For they considered not *the miracle* of the loaves; for their heart was hardened.

53 And when they had passed over, they came into the land of Gennesaret, and drew to the shore.

54 And when they were come out of the ship, straightway they knew him,

55 And ran through that whole region round about, and began to carry about in beds those that were sick, where they heard he was.

56 And whithersoever he entered, into villages, or cities, or country, they laid the sick in the streets, and besought him that they might touch if it were but the border of his garment: and as many as touched him were made whole.

CHAPTER VII.

THEN came together unto him the Pharisees, and certain of the scribes, which came from Jerusalem.

2 And when they saw some of his disciples eat bread with defiled, that is to say, with unwashen hands, they found fault.

3 For the Pharisees, and all the Jews, except they wash *their* hands oft, eat not, holding the tradition of the elders.

4 And *when they come* from the market, except they wash, they eat not. And many other things there be, which they have received to hold, *as* the washing of cups, and pots, brazen vessels, and of tables.

5 Then the Pharisees and scribes asked him, Why walk not thy disciples according to the tradition of the elders, but eat bread with unwashen hands?

了。

第七章

有法利賽人和幾個讀書人、從耶路撒冷來、聚集到耶穌面前、〔看見他門徒有人手不乾淨就是沒有洗手喫飯、便責備他們〕〔因爲法利賽人和猶太衆人都守古人所傳下來的規矩、若不淨淨的洗手、就不喫飯、從街市上同來、若不洗浴也不喫飯、還有許多別的規矩他們承接堅守、就是洗杯盞銅器和牀當下法利賽人和讀書人問耶穌說你的門徒爲甚麼不遵古人所傳下來的規矩、喫飯不先洗手呢。

於是上船到了他們那裏風就止住衆人心裏甚是驚訝希奇因爲他們心裏愚頑不明白分餅的奇事。○飯渡過去、到了革尼撒勒地方、將船泊在岸邊。他們下了船衆人就認得耶穌跑遍周圍地方聽見耶穌在那裏就將有病的人用牀擡到那裏。凡耶穌所到的地方、或村中、或城裏或鄉下人都將病人放在街市上只求耶穌容他們摸他的衣裳穗子、摸著的人就都好

6 He answered and said unto them; Well hath Esaias prophesied of you hypocrites, as it is written, This people honoureth me with *their* lips, but their heart is far from me.

7 Howbeit in vain do they worship me, teaching *for* doctrines the commandments of men.

8 For laying aside the commandment of God, ye hold the tradition of men, *as* the washing of pots and cups : and many other such like things ye do.

9 And he said unto them, Full well ye reject the commaudment of God, that ye may keep your own tradition.

10 For Moses said, Honour thy father and thy mother ; and, Whoso curseth father or mother, let him die the death :

11 But ye say, If a man shall say to his father or mother, *It is* Corban, that is to say, a gift, by whatsoever thou mightest be profited by me ; *he shall be free.*

12 And ye suffer him no more to do aught for his father or his mother ;

13 Making the word of God of none effect through your tradition, which ye have delivered : and many such like things do ye.

14 ¶ And when he had called all the people *unto him,* he said unto them, Hearken unto me every one *of you,* and understand :

15 There is nothing from without a man, that entering into him can defile him : but the things which come out of him, those are they that defile the man.

16 If any man have ears to hear, let him hear.

17 And when he was entered into the house from the people, his disciples asked him concerning the parable.

耶穌同答說以賽亞預先指著你們假冒爲善的人說的話是不錯的、他說這百姓用口尊敬我、心裏郤是遠離我、他們將人

所吩咐的、當作道理教訓人、所以拜我也是徒然的、你們丟棄 神的誡命、守著古人所傳下來的規矩、去洗杯爵盆盞你們還

做許多這樣的事、又說你們實在是廢了 神的誡命、守自己所承接的規矩、摩西曾說應當孝敬父母、又說咒罵父母的人、

必當治死他、你們倒說人若對父母說我所應當奉養給你的、巳經作了各爾板、各爾板繙出來、就是禮物、以後不事奉父母是

可以的、這就是你們不許他再事奉父母、因自己所承接的規矩廢了 神的道了、你們還做許多這樣的事、○ 耶穌叫衆人

前來、說、你們都當聽我的話、也要心裏明白、凡從外面進去的、不能污穢人、惟有從裏面出來的、纔能污穢人、凡有耳可聽的、

都應當聽。耶穌離了衆人、進屋子裏門徒來問道比喻的意思。

18 And he saith unto them, Are ye so without understanding also? Do ye not perceive, that whatsoever thing from without entereth into the man, *it* cannot defile him;

19 Because it entereth not into his heart, but into the belly, and goeth out into the draught, purging all meats?

20 And he said, That which cometh out of the man, that defileth the man.

21 For from within, out of the heart of men, proceed evil thoughts, adulteries, fornications, murders,

22 Thefts, covetousness, wickedness, deceit, lasciviousness, an evil eye, blasphemy, pride, foolishness:

23 All these evil things come from within, and defile the man.

24 ¶ And from thence he arose, and went into the borders of Tyre and Sidon, and entered into a house, and would have no man know *it*: but he could not be hid.

25 For a *certain* woman, whose young daughter had an unclean spirit, heard of him, and came and fell at his feet:

26 The woman was a Greek, a Syrophenician by nation; and she besought him that he would cast forth the devil out of her daughter.

27 But Jesus said unto her, Let the children first be filled: for it is not meet to take the children's bread, and to cast *it* unto the dogs.

28 And she answered and said unto him, Yes, Lord: yet the dogs under the table eat of the children's crumbs.

29 And he said unto her, For this saying go thy way; the devil is gone out of thy daughter.

30 And when she was come to her house, she found the devil gone out, and her daughter laid upon the bed.

31 ¶ And again, departing from the coasts of Tyre and Sidon, he came unto the sea of Galilee, through the midst of the coasts of Decapolis.

耶穌說、你們也這樣不明白麼、豈不曉得凡從外面進去的、不能污穢人、因為不是進他心裏去、乃是進他肚裏去、落到茅厠裏凡所喫的就乾淨了、又說從裏面出來的、這纔能污穢人、因為從人心裏出來的、就是惡念姦淫苟合兇殺、盜竊貪婪、邪惡詭詐、淫蕩嫉妬、謗讟驕傲狂妄、這一切不好的事、都是從裏面出來的、並且能污穢人。○耶穌從那裏起身、往推羅西頓的境內去、進入一家、不願人知道、邲不能隱藏、因為有一個婦人、他的女兒被邪鬼附著、聽見耶穌的事、就來俯伏在他脚前、這婦人是希利尼人、或作外邦人屬敍利非尼基族、他求耶穌趕鬼離開女兒、耶穌對他說、先容兒女喫飽、拏兒女的餅丟給狗喫、是不可以的。婦人回答說、主阿、是的、但狗在桌子底下、也喫兒女膔下的零碎。耶穌說、因這一句話、你回去罷、鬼已經離開你的女兒了。婦人回到自己家裏、就曉得鬼已經出去、看見女兒躺在牀上。○耶穌離了推羅西頓的地方、從低加波利境內經過、又到了加利利的海邊。

32 And they bring unto him one that was deaf, and had an impediment in his speech; and they beseech him to put his hand upon him.

33 And he took him aside from the multitude, and put his fingers into his ears, and he spit, and touched his tongue;

34 And looking up to heaven, he sighed, and saith unto him, Ephphatha, that is, Be opened.

35 And straightway his ears were opened, and the string of his tongue was loosed, and he spake plain.

36 And he charged them that they should tell no man: but the more he charged them, so much the more a great deal they published *it*;

37 And were beyond measure astonished, saying, He hath done all things well: he maketh both the deaf to hear, and the dumb to speak.

CHAPTER VIII.

IN those days the multitude being very great, and having nothing to eat, Jesus called his disciples *unto him*, and saith unto them,

2 I have compassion on the multitude, because they have now been with me three days, and have nothing to eat:

3 And if I send them away fasting to their own houses, they will faint by the way: for divers of them came from far.

4 And his disciples answered him, From whence can a man satisfy these *men* with bread here in the wilderness?

5 And he asked them, how many loaves have ye? And they said, Seven.

6 And he commanded the people to sit down on the ground: and he took the seven loaves, and gave thanks, and brake, and gave to his disciples to set before *them*; and they did set *them* before the people.

有人帶一個耳聾口吃的人、來見耶穌、求耶穌按手在他身上。耶穌領他離開衆人、到僻靜的地方、用手指探他的耳朶、用唾

沬抹他的舌頭、望天歎息、對他說以法大、繙出來、就是開了罷。那人的耳朶就開了、舌頭也舒展了、說話也清楚了。耶穌禁止

他們、不要告訴人只是越發禁止他們越發傳開了。衆人分外詫異說他所做的事都好、叫聾子能聽又叫啞吧能說話。

第八章

當那時候、有許多人在那裏沒有東西喫、耶穌叫了門徒來、對他們說、我憐憫這衆人、他們同我在這裏已經三日沒有東西

喫、我若叫他們餓著回家、必在道路上困乏、因爲內中有從遠處來的門徒說、在這曠野地方、從那裏得餅、叫這許多人喫飽

呢。耶穌問門徒說你們有多少餅。回答說七個。耶穌就吩咐衆人坐在地上、拏這七個餅、祝謝、擘開、遞給門徒叫他們擺設門

徒就擺設在衆人面前。

7 And they had a few small fishes: and he blessed, and commanded to set them also before *them*.

8 So they did eat, and were filled: and they took up of the broken *meat* that was left seven baskets.

9 And they that had eaten were about four thousand: and he sent them away.

10 ¶ And straightway he entered into a ship with his disciples, and came into the parts of Dalmanutha.

11 And the Pharisees came forth, and began to question with him, seeking of him a sign from heaven, tempting him.

12 And he sighed deeply in his spirit, and saith, Why doth this generation seek after a sign? verily I say unto you, There shall no sign be given unto this generation.

13 And he left them, and entering into the ship again departed to the other side.

14 ¶ Now *the disciples* had forgotten to take bread, neither had they in the ship with them more than one loaf.

15 And he charged them, saying, Take heed, beware of the leaven of the Pharisees, and *of* the leaven of Herod.

16 And they reasoned among themselves, saying, *It is* because we have no bread.

17 And when Jesus knew *it*, he saith unto them, Why reason ye, because ye have no bread? perceive ye not yet, neither understand? have ye your heart yet hardened?

18 Having eyes, see ye not? and having ears, hear ye not? and do ye not remember?

19 When I brake the five loaves among five thousand, how many baskets full of fragments took ye up? They say unto him, Twelve.

20 And when the seven among four thousand, how many baskets full of fragments took ye up? And they said, Seven.

還有幾尾小魚、耶穌又祝謝了叫擺設在眾人面前眾人都喫飽了收拾賸下的零碎裝滿了七個籃子喫的人約有四千耶

穌遣散了眾人、○就和門徒上船往大馬孥大地方去法利賽人出來盤問耶穌求耶穌從天上顯奇事與他們看意思要試

探他耶穌心裏歎息說這世代爲甚麼求奇事呢我實在告訴你們斷沒有奇事給這世代看○耶穌就離開他們又上船渡到

那邊岸上去了○門徒忘了帶餅在船上除了一個餅沒有別的食物耶穌微戒他們說應當謹防法利賽人的酵和希律的

酵。○門徒彼此議論說這是因爲我們沒有帶餅罷耶穌曉得就說爲甚麼因爲沒有帶餅彼此議論呢你們還不省悟不明白

麼心裏還是愚頑麼你們有眼看不見麼有耳聾不見麼也不記得麼我擘開五個餅分給五千人、你們收拾零碎裝滿了幾

個籃子。回答說、十二個。我擘開七個餅分給四千人、你們收拾零碎裝滿了幾個籃子。回答說七個。

21 And he said unto them, How is it that ye do not understand?

22 ¶ And he cometh to Bethsaida; and they bring a blind man unto him, and besought him to touch him.

23 And he took the blind man by the hand, and led him out of the town; and when he had spit on his eyes, and put his hands upon him, he asked him if he saw aught.

24 And he looked up, and said, I see men as trees, walking.

25 After that he put *his* hands again upon his eyes, and made him look up; and he was restored, and saw every man clearly.

26 And he sent him away to his house, saying, Neither go into the town, nor tell *it* to any in the town.

27 ¶ And Jesus went out, and his disciples, into the towns of Cesarea Philippi: and by the way he asked his disciples, saying unto them, Whom do men say that I am?

28 And they answered, John the Baptist: but some *say*, Elias; and others, One of the prophets.

29 And he saith unto them, But whom say ye that I am? And Peter answereth and saith unto him, Thou art the Christ.

30 And he charged them that they should tell no man of him.

31 And he began to teach them, that the Son of Man must suffer many things, and be rejected of the elders, and *of* the chief priests, and scribes, and be killed, and after three days rise again.

32 And he spake that saying openly. And Peter took him, and began to rebuke him.

33 But when he had turned about and looked on his disciples, he rebuked Peter, saying, Get thee behind me, Satan: for thou savourest not the things that be of God, but the things that be of men.

就對他們說、你們怎麼還不明白呢。○耶穌到了百賽大有人帶一個瞎子來、求耶穌摸他耶穌拉著瞎子的手、領他到村外、

吐唾沫在他眼睛上、又用手按他、問他看見甚麼沒有。瞎子就望上看、說我看見行走的人彷彿樹木一般耶穌又按手在他

眼睛上、叫他再望上看、就痊愈了、各樣東西、都看得明白耶穌打發他囘家說、不可進村子裏去也不可告訴村裏的人。○耶

穌和門徒、往該撒利亞腓力比的各村莊去、路上問門徒說人說我是誰囘答說有人說是施洗的約翰有人說是以利亞又

有人說是先知裏的一位耶穌說你們說我是誰。彼得說你是　基督耶穌切切的禁戒他們、不可告訴人。○於是教訓他們

說人子必受許多的苦、被衆長老祭司長和讀書人厭棄還要被殺過三日必要復活耶穌明明白白的說這話彼得就拉著

他、勸他。耶穌轉身看著門徒、責備彼得說撒但、退去罷、因爲你不體貼　神的意思只體貼人的意思。

34 ¶ And when he had called the people *unto him* with his disciples also, he said unto them, Whosoever will come after me, let him deny himself, and take up his cross, and follow me.

35 For whosoever will save his life shall lose it; but whosoever shall lose his life for my sake and the gospel's, the same shall save it.

36 For what shall it profit a man, if he shall gain the whole world, and lose his own soul?

37 Or what shall a man give in exchange for his soul?

38 Whosoever therefore shall be ashamed of me and of my words, in this adulterous and sinful generation, of him also shall the Son of man be ashamed, when he cometh in the glory of his Father with the holy angels.

CHAPTER IX.

AND he said unto them, Verily I say unto you, That there be some of them that stand here, which shall not taste of death, till they have seen the kingdom of God come with power.

2 ¶ And after six days Jesus taketh *with him* Peter, and James, and John; and leadeth them up into a high mountain apart by themselves: and he was transfigured before them.

3 And his raiment became shining, exceeding white as snow; so as no fuller on earth can white them.

4 And there appeared unto them Elias with Moses: and they were talking with Jesus.

5 And Peter answered and said to Jesus, Master, it is good for us to be here: and let us make three tabernacles; one for thee, and one for Moses, and one for Elias.

6 For he wist not what to say; for they were sore afraid.

○耶穌叫衆人和門徒來、對他們說、有人要跟從我、就當克己、背著十字架跟從我。凡要保全生命的、必喪掉生命、凡爲我和福音的道理喪掉生命的、必保全天下的財利、喪掉生命、靈魂作有甚麼益處。人能拏甚麼來換生命、或靈魂呢。凡在這姦淫作惡的世代、將我和我的道理當作可恥的、人子得了天父的榮耀同聖天使降臨的時候、也必將那人當作可恥的。

第九章

耶穌又説我實在告訴你們、站在這裏的、有人在未死以前、必要看見 神的國、大有威權臨到。○過了六日耶穌帶著彼得、雅各約翰暗暗的上了高山、在他們面前改變形像、他的衣服光亮、極白如雪、世上漂布的人、不能漂得這樣白、忽有摩西以利亞、在他們面前顯現、和耶穌説話、彼得對耶穌説、夫子、我們在這裏最好容我們搭三座棚、一座爲你、一座爲摩西、一座爲以利亞。彼得説這話、邥不知道説的是甚麼因爲三個人都懼怕。

7 And there was a cloud that over-shadowed them : and a voice came out of the cloud, saying, This is my beloved Son : hear him.

8 And suddenly, when they had looked round about, they saw no man any more, save Jesus only with themselves.

9 And as they came down from the mountain, he charged them that they should tell no man what things they had seen, till the Son of man were risen from the dead.

10 And they kept that saying with themselves, questioning one with another what the rising from the dead should mean.

11 ¶ And they asked him, saying, Why say the scribes that Elias must first come ?

12 And he answered and told them, Elias verily cometh first, and restoreth all things ; and how it is written of the Son of man, that he must suffer many things, and be set at nought.

13 But I say unto you, That Elias is indeed come, and they have done unto him whatsoever they listed, as it is written of him.

14 ¶ And when he came to *his* disciples, he saw a great multitude about them, and the scribes question-ing with them.

15 And straightway all the people, when they beheld him, were greatly amazed, and running to *him* saluted him.

16 And he asked the scribes, What question ye with them ?

17 And one of the multitude an-swered and said, Master, I have brought unto thee my son, which hath a dumb spirit ;

18 And wheresoever he taketh him, he teareth him ; and he foameth, and gnasheth with his teeth, and pineth away : and I spake to thy disciples that they should cast him out ; and they could not.

有雲遮住他們、有聲音從雲裏出來說這是我的愛子、你們應當聽他。門徒忽然周圍一看、不見一人只有耶穌和他們自己

在那裏下山的時候耶穌囑咐他們說人子還沒有從死裏復活你們不可將所看見的告訴人門徒將這話記在心裏彼此

議論說從死裏復活是甚麼意思呢就問耶穌說讀書人爲甚麼說以利亞必須先來耶穌囘答說以利亞自然先來、整理萬

事、經上說、人子必受許多的苦害被人輕慢我告訴你們、以利亞已經來了人都任意待他應了經上指著他所說的話。○耶

穌到了門徒那裏看見有許多人圍繞他們、又有讀書人和他們辨論衆人一見耶穌就大大的詫異跑上去與他請安耶穌

問讀書人說你們和他們辨論是甚麼衆人中間有一人囘答說夫子我帶著我兒子來見你他被啞吧的鬼附著無論在那

裏鬼捉弄他、就將他推倒叫他口中流沫、齩牙切齒、身子枯乾我曾請你的門徒逐出這鬼、他們郤是不能。

19 He answereth him, and saith, O faithless generation, how long shall I be with you? how long shall I suffer you? bring him unto me.

20 And they brought him unto him: and when he saw him, straightway the spirit tare him; and he fell on the ground, and wallowed foaming.

21 And he asked his father, How long is it ago since this came unto him? And he said, Of a child.

22 And ofttimes it hath cast him into the fire, and into the waters, to destroy. him: but if thou canst do any thing, have compassion on us, and help us.

23 Jesus said unto him, If thou canst believe, all things *are* possible to him that believeth.

24 And straightway the father of the child cried out, and said with tears, Lord, I believe; help thou mine unbelief.

25 When Jesus saw that the people came running together, he rebuked the foul spirit, saying unto him, *Thou* dumb and deaf spirit, I charge thee, come out of him, and enter no more into him.

26 And *the spirit* cried, and rent him sore, and came out of him: and he was as one dead; insomuch that many said, He is dead.

27 But Jesus took him by the hand, and lifted him up; and he arose.

28 And when he was come into the house, his disciples asked him privately, Why could not we cast him out?

29 And he said unto them, This kind can come forth by nothing, but by prayer and fasting.

30 ¶ And they departed thence, and passed through Galilee; and he would not that any man should know *it*.

耶穌回答說這不信的世代我在你們這裏到幾時呢我忍耐你們到幾時呢將孩子帶到我這裏來那人就帶孩子前來一見

耶穌鬼就叫他抽了一陣瘋跌倒在地翻來覆去口流涎沫耶穌問他父親說他患這病有多少時候呢回答說從小時候

屢次叫他跌在火裏水裏要害死他你若能作這事就憐憫我們救濟我們耶穌說你若能信在信的人凡事沒有不能的

子的父親就流淚喊叫說主阿我信但我的信不足求你輔助耶穌看見衆人跑上來就震嚇邪鬼說聾啞的鬼我吩咐你從

他裏頭出來不許再進去那鬼喊叫使孩子大大的抽了一陣瘋就出來了孩子如同死了一般有許多人說他是已經死了

耶穌拉著孩子的手扶他起來孩子就站起來了耶穌進了屋子門徒暗暗的問他說我們爲甚麼不能逐出這鬼呢耶穌說

這一類的鬼若不禱告禁食總不能趕他出去。○以後他們離開那地方經過加利利耶穌不願人知道

31 For he taught his disciples, and said unto them, The Son of man is delivered into the hands of men, and they shall kill him; and after that he is killed, he shall rise the third day.

32 But they understood not that saying, and were afraid to ask him.

33 ¶ And he came to Capernaum: and being in the house he asked them, What was it that ye disputed among yourselves by the way?

34 But they held their peace: for by the way they had disputed among themselves, who *should be* the greatest.

35 And he sat down, and called the twelve, and saith unto them, If any man desire to be first, *the same* shall be last of all, and servant of all.

36 And he took a child, and set him in the midst of them: and when he had taken him in his arms, he said unto them,

37 Whosoever shall receive one of such children in my name, receiveth me; and whosoever shall receive me, receiveth not me, but him that sent me.

38 ¶ And John answered him, saying, Master, we saw one casting out devils in thy name, and he followeth not us; and we forbade him, because he followeth not us.

39 But Jesus said, Forbid him not: for there is no man which shall do a miracle in my name, that can lightly speak evil of me.

40 For he that is not against us is on our part.

41 For whosoever shall give you a cup of water to drink in my name, because ye belong to Christ, verily I say unto you, he shall not lose his reward.

42 And whosoever shall offend one of *these* little ones that believe in me, it is better for him that a millstone were hanged about his neck, and he were cast into the sea.

就告訴門徒說人子將要被賣到人手裏、爲人所殺、殺後第三日必要復活。門徒不明白這話、又不敢問他。○耶穌到了迦百農、在屋裏問門徒說、你們在路上彼此議論甚麼、門徒不作聲、因爲在路上彼此議論的、是誰爲大、耶穌坐下、叫十二個門徒來、對他們說、凡要做首先的、必要落在衆人末後、服事衆人、就拉著一個小孩子叫他站在門徒中間、又抱著他、對門徒說、凡爲我的名、接待一個像小孩子這樣的人、就是接待我、凡接待我、是接待差我來的父。○約翰對耶穌說、夫子、我們看見一個不跟從我們的人、奉你的名趕鬼、我們就禁止他、因爲他不跟從我們、耶穌說、不要禁止他、因爲沒有人奉我的名施行異能、反倒輕易毀謗我、凡不與我們爲敵的、就是順從我們的、凡爲我的名、擎一杯水給你們喝、因爲你們是屬基督的、我實在告訴你們、那人必不失掉他的賞賜、凡叫信我的一個小子陷在罪裏這人倒不如將磨盤石拴在頸項上、投在海裏。

43 And if thy hand offend thee, cut it off; it is better for thee to enter into life maimed, than having two hands to go into hell, into the fire that never shall be quenched:

44 Where their worm dieth not, and the fire is not quenched.

45 And if thy foot offend thee, cut it off: it is better for thee to enter halt into life, than having two feet to be cast into hell, into the fire that never shall be quenched:

46 Where their worm dieth not, and the fire is not quenched.

47 And if thine eye offend thee, pluck it out: it is better for thee to enter into the kingdom of God with one eye, than having two eyes to be cast into hell fire:

48 Where their worm dieth not, and the fire is not quenched.

49 For every one shall be salted with fire, and every sacrifice shall be salted with salt.

50 Salt *is* good: but if the salt have lost his saltness, wherewith will ye season it? Have salt in yourselves, and have peace one with another.

CHAPTER X.

AND he arose from thence, and cometh into the coasts of Judea by the farther side of Jordan: and the people resort unto him again; and, as he was wont, he taught them again.

2 ¶ And the Pharisees came to him, and asked him, Is it lawful for a man to put away *his* wife? tempting him.

3 And he answered and said unto them, What did Moses command you?

4 And they said, Moses suffered to write a bill of divorcement, and to put *her* away.

5 And Jesus answered and said unto them, For the hardness of your heart he wrote you this precept.

倘若你一隻手叫你犯罪就砍斷了你、短一隻手進入永生強如有兩隻手落到地獄不滅的火裏、那裏蟲是不死的火是不滅的。倘若你一隻脚叫你犯罪就砍斷了你、短一隻脚進入永生強如有兩隻脚落到地獄不滅的火裏、那裏蟲是不死的火是不滅的。倘若你一隻眼叫你犯罪就挖出來、你短一隻眼進入　神的國強如有兩隻眼落到地獄的火裏、那裏蟲是不死的火是不滅的因為凡人必被火煉凡祭物必用鹽醃鹽本是好的鹽若失了味、如何能叫這鹽再鹹呢你們裏面應當有鹽、也當彼此和睦。

第十章

耶穌從那裏起身、經過約但河外入了猶太的境內、衆人又聚集來見他、耶穌照常敎訓他們。法利賽人來問耶穌說、人休妻可以不可以、意思要試探他。耶穌回答說、摩西怎樣吩附你們、他們說、摩西吩附我們、寫了休書纔可以休妻耶穌說、摩西因為你們心裏剛硬、與你們留下這條例。

6 But from the beginning of the creation God made them male and female.

7 For this cause shall a man leave his father and mother, and cleave to his wife;

8 And they twain shall be one flesh: so then they are no more twain, but one flesh.

9 What therefore God hath joined together, let not man put asunder.

10 And in the house his disciples asked him again of the same *matter.*

11 And he saith unto them, Whosoever shall put away his wife, and marry another, committeth adultery against her.

12 And if a woman shall put away her husband, and be married to another, she committeth adultery.

13 ¶ And they brought young children to him, that he should touch them; and *his* disciples rebuked those that brought *them.*

14 But when Jesus saw *it,* he was much displeased, and said unto them, Suffer the little children to come unto me, and forbid them not; for of such is the kingdom of God.

15 Verily I say unto you, Whosoever shall not receive the kingdom of God as a little child, he shall not enter therein.

16 And he took them up in his arms, put *his* hands upon them, and blessed them.

17 ¶ And when he was gone forth into the way, there came one running, and kneeled to him, and asked him, Good Master, what shall I do that I may inherit eternal life?

18 And Jesus said unto him, Why callest thou me good? *there is* none good but one, *that is,* God.

19 Thou knowest the commandments, Do not commit adultery, Do not kill, Do not steal, Do not bear false witness, Defraud not, Honour thy father and mother.

其實起初造萬物的時候、神造人是造一男一女因此人要離開父母、與妻子如膠似漆兩人成爲一體這樣看來、夫妻不

再算是兩個人乃算是一體的了所以　神所配合的人不可以分開到了屋裏門徒也將這事問他耶穌回答說凡休妻另

娶就是犯了姦淫寧負妻子妻子若離棄丈夫另嫁也是犯了姦淫〇有人帶著小孩子來見耶穌要耶穌摸他們門徒責備

那帶小孩子來的人耶穌看見就不喜悅、對門徒說容小孩子到我這裏來不要禁止因爲在　神國的正是像小孩子這樣

的人我實在告訴你們凡要承受　神國的若不像小孩子的樣子必不得進去就抱著小孩子按手在他們頭上爲他們祝

福。〇耶穌出來行路的時候有一個人跑來跪在他面前問他說良善的夫子我當行甚麼事纔能得永生耶穌說你爲甚麼

釋我是良善的除了　神沒有一個良善的。

20 And he answered and said unto him, Master, all these have I observed from my youth.

21 Then Jesus beholding him loved him, and said unto him, One thing thou lackest: go thy way, sell whatsoever thou hast, and give to the poor, and thou shalt have treasure in heaven: and come, take up the cross, and follow me.

22 And he was sad at that saying, and went away grieved: for he had great possessions.

23 ¶ And Jesus looked round about, and saith unto his disciples, How hardly shall they that have riches enter into the kingdom of God!

24 And the disciples were astonished at his words. But Jesus answereth again, and saith unto them, Children, how hard is it for them that trust in riches to enter into the kingdom of God!

25 It is easier for a camel to go through the eye of a needle, than for a rich man to enter into the kingdom of God.

26 And they were astonished out of measure, saying among themselves, Who then can be saved?

27 And Jesus looking upon them saith, With men it is impossible, but not with God: for with God all things are possible.

28 ¶ Then Peter began to say unto him, Lo, we have left all, and have followed thee.

29 And Jesus answered and said, Verily I say unto you, There is no man that hath left house, or brethren, or sisters, or father, or mother, or wife, or children, or lands, for my sake, and the gospel's,

30 But he shall receive a hundredfold now in this time, houses, and brethren, and sisters, and mothers, and children, and lands, with persecutions; and in the world to come eternal life.

誡命你是曉得的、卽如不可姦淫、不可殺人、不可偷盜、不可妄作見證、不可拐騙人、要孝敬父母。那人囘答說夫子這些誡命

我從小時候都遵守了。耶穌看著那人就愛惜他對他說你還缺少一樣、你去賣了你所有的、賙濟窮人、就必有財寶在天上、

又當負著十字架來跟從我。那人聽見這話就變了顏色、愛愛愁愁的去了、因爲他的產業甚多。耶穌周圍一看、對門徒說有

錢財的人進 神的國眞是難哪。門徒詫異他的話、耶穌又說、小子倚靠錢財的人進 神的國眞是難哪、駱駝穿過鍼的眼、

比財主進 神的國還容易呢。門徒甚詫異、彼此說這樣、誰能得救呢。耶穌看著他們說、在 神就不然、因爲

神是沒有不能的。彼得對耶穌說我們已經撒下一切所有的、跟從你了。耶穌囘答說、我實在告訴你們、凡爲我和福音撒

下家宅弟兄姐妹父母妻子兒女田地的、必在今世得百倍就是家宅弟兄姐妹母親兒女田地並且要受逼迫、到來世必得

永生。

31 But many *that are* first shall be last; and the last first.

32 ¶ And they were in the way going up to Jerusalem; and Jesus went before them: and they were amazed; and as they followed, they were afraid. And he took again the twelve, and began to tell them what things should happen unto him,

33 *Saying*, Behold, we go up to Jerusalem; and the Son of Man shall be delivered unto the chief priests, and unto the scribes; and they shall condemn him to death, and shall deliver him to the Gentiles:

34 And they shall mock him, and shall scourge him, and shall spit upon him, and shall kill him; and the third day he shall rise again.

35 ¶ And James and John, the sons of Zebedee, come unto him, saying, Master, we would that thou shouldest do for us whatsoever we shall desire.

36 And he said unto them, What would ye that I should do for you?

37 They said unto him, Grant unto us that we may sit, one on thy right hand, and the other on thy left hand, in thy glory.

38 But Jesus said unto them, Ye know not what ye ask: can ye drink of the cup that I drink of? and be baptized with the baptism that I am baptized with?

39 And they said unto him, We can. And Jesus said unto them, Ye shall indeed drink of the cup that I drink of; and with the baptism that I am baptized withal shall ye be baptized:

40 But to sit on my right hand and on my left hand is not mine to give; but *it shall be given to them* for whom it is prepared.

41 And when the ten heard *it*, they began to be much displeased with James and John.

然而有許多在前的將要在後、在後的將要在前了。○他們行路上耶路撒冷去、耶穌在前面走、門徒跟隨他、又詫異又懼怕、

耶穌叫了十二個門徒來、再將自己要遇見的事告訴他們、說我們上耶路撒冷人子將被賣給祭司長和讀書人、他們要定

他死罪、解交外邦人凌辱他、鞭打他、吐唾沫在他身上、殺害他、第三日他必復活。○西庇太的兒子雅各約翰、來見耶穌說、夫

子、我們無論求你甚麼要你爲我們成就、耶穌說要我爲你們做甚麼呢、囘答說你得榮耀的時候、許我們一個坐在你右邊、

一個坐在你左邊、耶穌說你們所求的、自己不知道、我將喝的那一杯、你們能喝麼、我將受的洗、你們能受麼。囘答說我們能。

耶穌說我所喝的那一杯、你們也必要喝、我所受的洗、你們也必要受、只是坐在我的左右、不是我可以賜的、乃是預備給誰、

我我字無就賜給誰。十二個門徒聽見就惱怒雅各約翰。

42 But Jesus called them *to him*, and saith unto them, Ye know that they which are accounted to rule over the Gentiles exercise lordship over them; and their great ones exercise authority upon them.

43 But so shall it not be among you: but whosoever will be great among you, shall be your minister:

44 And whosoever of you will be the chiefest, shall be servant of all.

45 For even the Son of Man came not to be ministered unto, but to minister, and to give his life a ransom for many.

46 ¶ And they came to Jericho: and as he went out of Jericho with his disciples and a great number of people, blind Bartimeus, the son of Timeus, sat by the highway side begging.

47 And when he heard that it was Jesus of Nazareth, he began to cry out, and say, Jesus, *thou* Son of David, have mercy on me.

48 And many charged him that he should hold his peace: but he cried the more a great deal, *Thou* Son of David, have mercy on me.

49 And Jesus stood still, and commanded him to be called. And they call the blind man, saying unto him, Be of good comfort, rise; he calleth thee.

50 And he, casting away his garment, rose, and came to Jesus.

51 And Jesus answered and said unto him, What wilt thou that I should do unto thee? The blind man said unto him, Lord, that I might receive my sight.

52 And Jesus said unto him, Go thy way; thy faith hath made thee whole. And immediately he received his sight, and followed Jesus in the way.

耶穌叫了他們來說、外邦人有君王管束他們、有大臣轄制他們、這是你們知道的、只是你們中間不可這樣、你們中間誰要為大、

就當服事你們、誰要居首位、就當作你們衆人的僕人、因為人子來、並不是要受人的服事、乃是要服事人、並且捨命替衆人

贖罪。○後來到了耶利哥、耶穌同著門徒和許多人出耶利哥的時候有一個瞎子巴底買是底買的兒子坐在道旁討飯。

見是拏撒勒的耶穌就喊叫說大闢的子孫耶穌憐恤我、衆人責備他、不許他嗄嚷、他越發喊叫說、大闢的子孫憐恤我、耶穌

站住、吩咐人叫他來、人就去叫那瞎子對他說你放心起來、主叫你、瞎子丟下衣服起來、到耶穌面前、耶穌對他說你要我

為你作甚麼瞎子回答說拉波尼、卽我夫子我意夫要能看見、耶穌說你去罷、你的信救了你了、瞎子就看見了、在路上跟隨耶穌

CHAPTER XI.

AND when they came nigh to Jerusalem, unto Bethphage and Bethany, at the mount of Olives, he sendeth forth two of his disciples,

2 And saith unto them, Go your way into the village over against you: and as soon as ye be entered into it, ye shall find a colt tied, whereon never man sat; loose him, and bring *him*.

3 And if any man say unto you, Why do ye this? say ye that the Lord hath need of him; and straightway he will send him hither.

4 And they went their way, and found the colt tied by the door without in a place where two ways met; and they loose him.

5 And certain of them that stood there said unto them, What do ye, loosing the colt?

6 And they said unto them even as Jesus had commanded: and they let them go.

7 And they brought the colt to Jesus, and cast their garments on him; and he sat upon him.

8 And many spread their garments in the way; and others cut down branches off the trees, and strewed *them* in the way.

9 And they that went before, and they that followed, cried, saying, Hosanna; Blessed *is* he that cometh in the name of the Lord:

10 Blessed *be* the kingdom of our father David, that cometh in the name of the Lord: Hosanna in the highest.

11 And Jesus entered into Jerusalem, and into the temple: and when he had looked round about upon all things, and now the eventide was come, he went out unto Bethany with the twelve.

12 ¶ And on the morrow, when they were come from Bethany, he was hungry:

第十一章

耶穌和門徒將近耶路撒冷先到了靠橄欖山的伯法其伯大尼耶穌差遣兩個門徒對他們說你們往對面村莊去進去的時候必要看見那裏拴著一個沒有人騎過的驢駒你們可以解開牽到我這裏來若有人問你們為甚麼解驢就說主要用他那人必要叫你們牽來。門徒去了果然看見驢駒拴在門外岔路口上就將他解開在那裏站著的人有幾個問他們說解驢作甚麼門徒按著耶穌所吩咐的話回答那些人就由他們去了他們牽了驢駒到耶穌這裏來將自己的衣服搭在上面。耶穌就騎上了。有許多人將自己的衣服鋪在道路上也有人砍下樹枝來鋪在道路上並且前前後後的人都大聲說和散那、即求救率　主的名來的、是應當稱頌的、我祖大闢的國奉　主的名而來、是應當稱頌的、在至上之處、當稱和散那耶穌到了耶路撒冷進了聖殿周圍觀看殿中各物、時候已經晚了、就和十二個門徒出來、往伯大尼去了。○次日、離了伯大尼耶穌餓了。

13 And seeing a fig tree afar off having leaves, he came, if haply he might find any thing thereon: and when he came to it, he found nothing but leaves; for the time of figs was not *yet*.

14 And Jesus answered and said unto it, No man eat fruit of thee hereafter for ever. And his disciples heard *it*.

15 ¶ And they come to Jerusalem: and Jesus went into the temple, and began to cast out them that sold and bought in the temple, and overthrew the tables of the money changers, and the seats of them that sold doves;

16 And would not suffer that any man should carry *any* vessel through the temple.

17 And he taught, saying unto them, Is it not written, My house shall be called of all nations the house of prayer? but ye have made it a den of thieves.

18 And the scribes and chief priests heard *it*, and sought how they might destroy him: for they feared him, because all the people was astonished at his doctrine.

19 And when even was come, he went out of the city.

20 ¶ And in the morning, as they passed by, they saw the fig tree dried up from the roots.

21 And Peter calling to remembrance saith unto him, Master, behold, the fig tree which thou cursedst is withered away.

22 And Jesus answering saith unto them, Have faith in God.

23 For verily I say unto you, That whosoever shall say unto this mountain, Be thou removed, and be thou cast into the sea; and shall not doubt in his heart, but shall believe that those things which he saith shall come to pass; he shall have whatsoever he saith.

遠遠看見一棵無花果樹、樹上有葉子就往前來想在樹上得果子到了樹下、找不著甚麼、只有葉子因爲結果子的時候還

沒有到。〔耶穌對樹說從今以後你永遠不能結果子給人喫、門徒都聽見了。〇他們來到耶路撒冷耶穌進入聖殿裏面作

買賣的人趕出去推倒兌換銀錢的人的桌子、和賣鴿子的人的凳子又不許人擎器具從聖殿經過、教訓他們說經上不是

說、我的殿必稱爲萬國禱告的地方麼、你們竟將這殿當作盜賊的巢穴了。讓書人和衆祭司長聽見這話就圖謀要殺害他、

鄰又懼怕因爲衆人以他的教訓爲希奇。〇到了晚上耶穌出城去次日早晨他們從無花果樹下經過、看見樹連根都枯乾

了。〔彼得想起耶穌的話就說夫子請看你所呪詛的無花果樹已經枯乾了。〔耶穌回答說你們應當信服

神我實在告訴你

們、無論何人對這座山說離開此處、投在海裏心裏沒有疑惑、深信所說的必成、所說的就必給他成了。

24 Therefore I say unto you, What things soever ye desire, when ye pray, believe that ye receive *them*, and ye shall have *them*.

25 And when ye stand praying, forgive, if ye have aught against any; that your Father also which is in heaven may forgive you your trespasses.

26 But if ye do not forgive, neither will your Father which is in heaven forgive your trespasses.

27 ¶ And they come again to Jerusalem: and as he was walking in the temple, there come to him the chief priests, and the scribes, and the elders,

28 And say unto him, By what authority doest thou these things? and who gave thee this authority to do these things?

29 And Jesus answered and said unto them, I will also ask of you one question, and answer me, and I will tell you by what authority I do these things.

30 The baptism of John, was *it* from heaven, or of men? answer me.

31 And they reasoned with themselves, saying, If we shall say, From heaven; he will say, Why then did ye not believe him?

32 But if we shall say, Of men; they feared the people: for all *men* counted John, that he was a prophet indeed.

33 And they answered and said unto Jesus, We cannot tell. And Jesus answering saith unto them, Neither do I tell you by what authority I do these things.

CHAPTER XII.

AND he began to speak unto them by parables. A *certain* man planted a vineyard, and set a hedge about *it*, and digged *a place for* the winefat, and built a tower, and let it out to husbandmen, and went into a far country.

事。

第十二章

耶穌用比喻對衆人說、有一個人種葡萄園、周圍圈上籬笆、裏面挖一個壓酒處、造一座樓、租給園戶、就往別處去了。

我所以對你們說祈禱的時候無論求甚麼只要信我必得著、就必得著了〇你們站著祈禱若想起有人得罪你就當饒恕他、

你們在天上的父、也必饒恕你們的罪過。你們若不饒恕人、你們在天上的父、也不饒恕你們的罪過〇他們又到了耶路撒

冷耶穌在聖殿行走的時候衆祭司長和讀書人並長老都到他面前來、對他說、你用甚麼權柄作這些事、誰賜你權柄作這

些事呢。耶穌回答說、我也有一句話問你們你們若是告訴我我就告訴你們我用甚麼權柄作這些事。約翰的洗禮、是從天

上來的、還是從人間來的你們同答我。他們私下議論說我們若說從天上來、他必說、爲甚麼不信他。我們若說從人間來、卻

懼怕百姓因爲衆人都以爲約翰實在是先知就同答耶穌說我們不曉得耶穌說我也不告訴你們我用甚麼權柄作這些

2 And at the season he sent to the husbandmen a servant, that he might receive from the husbandmen of the fruit of the vineyard.

3 And they caught *him*, and beat him, and sent *him* away empty.

4 And again he sent unto them another servant; and at him they cast stones, and wounded *him* in the head, and sent *him* away shamefully handled.

5 And again he sent another; and him they killed, and many others; beating some, and killing some.

6 Having yet therefore one son, his well beloved, he sent him also last unto them, saying, They will reverence my son.

7 But those husbandmen said among themselves, This is the heir; come, let us kill him, and the inheritance shall be ours.

8 And they took him, and killed *him*, and cast *him* out of the vineyard.

9 What shall therefore the lord of the vineyard do? he will come and destroy the husbandmen, and will give the vineyard unto others.

10 And have ye not read this Scripture; The stone which the builders rejected is become the head of the corner:

11 This was the Lord's doing, and it is marvellous in our eyes?

12 And they sought to lay hold on him, but feared the people; for they knew that he had spoken the parable against them: and they left him, and went their way.

13 ¶ And they send unto him certain of the Pharisees and of the Herodians, to catch him in *his* words.

14 And when they were come, they say unto him, Master, we know that thou art true, and carest for no man; for thou regardest not the person of men, but teachest the way of God in truth: Is it lawful to give tribute to Cesar, or not?

到了日期打發一個僕人到了園戶那裏要從園戶手裏收葡萄園的果子園戶拏住打了他叫他空手回去又打發別的僕人去園戶拏石頭砍傷他的頭、又淩辱他叫他問去、以後又打發一個僕人去園戶殺了他、再打發許多僕人去、有被他們打的、有被他們殺的園主還有一個愛子末後打發他去以爲他們必要尊敬我的兒子了園戶彼此說這是承接產業的我們不如殺了他產業必歸我們了就拏住殺了他擡在園外葡萄園的主人將怎樣辦理呢、他必要來滅那園戶將園子租給別人、經上說工匠所廢棄的石頭作了房角的頭塊石頭這是　主所作的、在我們眼睛裏甚覺希奇這經你們沒有讀過麼他們曉得這比喻是指著他們自己說的、想要提住耶穌又懼怕百姓、就離開他去了。○後來打發幾個法利賽人並幾個希律一黨的人去要就著耶穌所說的話陷害他那些人來對耶穌說夫子我們曉得你是誠實的是不徇情待人的因爲你不是看外貌取人、乃是用誠實傳　神的道、納稅給該撒應當不應當

15 Shall we give, or shall we not give? But he, knowing their hypocrisy, said unto them, Why tempt ye me? bring me a penny, that I may see *it*.

16 And they brought *it*. And he saith unto them, Whose *is* this image and superscription? And they said unto him, Cesar's.

17 And Jesus answering said unto them, Render to Cesar the things that are Cesar's, and to God the things that are God's. And they marvelled at him.

18 ¶ Then come unto him the Sadducees, which say there is no resurrection; and they asked him, saying,

19 Master, Moses wrote unto us, If a man's brother die, and leave *his* wife *behind him*, and leave no children, that his brother should take his wife, and raise up seed unto his brother.

20 Now there were seven brethren: and the first took a wife, and dying left no seed.

21 And the second took her, and died, neither left he any seed: and the third likewise.

22 And the seven had her, and left no seed: last of all the woman died also.

23 In the resurrection therefore, when they shall rise, whose wife shall she be of them? for the seven had her to wife.

24 And Jesus answering said unto them, Do ye not therefore err, because ye know not the Scriptures, neither the power of God?

25 For when they shall rise from the dead, they neither marry, nor are given in marriage; but are as the angels which are in heaven.

26 And as touching the dead, that they rise; have ye not read in the book of Moses, how in the bush God spake unto him, saying, I *am* the God of Abraham, and the God of Isaac, and the God of Jacob?

可交納不可交納。耶穌曉得他們的假意就說你們爲甚麼試探我拿一個銀錢來給我看他們就拿了來。耶穌說這像和這號是誰的。回答說是該撒的。耶穌說該撒的東西當歸給該撒　神的東西當歸給　神衆人甚以爲希奇。○撒都該人常就

人死不能復活他們有幾個人來見耶穌說夫子摩西在書上曉諭我們說人若死了沒有兒子留下妻子他兄弟應當娶他的妻子生兒子承繼哥哥有弟兄七個人居長的娶了妻子死了沒有留下兒子第二個也是這樣那七個人都娶過他總沒有留下兒末後那婦人也死了七個人旣都娶過他、到復活的時候他們都

復活這婦人算是誰的妻子呢。耶穌回答說你們不明白聖經也不明白　神的大能、竟這樣說豈不是錯了麼。復活之後人

都不嫁不娶、如同天上的使者一樣。論到死人復活、你們沒有讀過摩西的書荊棘篇上所載的話麼那篇上記著　神對摩

西說我是亞伯拉罕的　神以撒的　神雅各的　神、

27 He is not the God of the dead, but the God of the living: ye therefore do greatly err.

28 ¶ And one of the scribes came, and having heard them reasoning together, and perceiving that he had answered them well, asked him, Which is the first commandment of all?

29 And Jesus answered him, The first of all the commandments is, Hear, O Israel; The Lord our God is one Lord:

30 And thou shalt love the Lord thy God with all thy heart, and with all thy soul, and with all thy mind, and with all thy strength: this is the first commandment.

31 And the second is like, namely this, Thou shalt love thy neighbour as thyself. There is none other commandment greater than these.

32 And the scribe said unto him, Well, Master, thou hast said the truth: for there is one God; and there is none other but he:

33 And to love him with all the heart, and with all the understanding, and with all the soul, and with all the strength, and to love his neighbour as himself, is more than all whole burnt offerings and sacrifices.

34 And when Jesus saw that he answered discreetly, he said unto him, Thou art not far from the kingdom of God. And no man after that durst ask him any question.

35 ¶ And Jesus answered and said, while he taught in the temple, How say the scribes that Christ is the son of David?

36 For David himself said by the Holy Ghost, The LORD said to my Lord, Sit thou on my right hand, till I make thine enemies thy footstool.

37 David therefore himself calleth him Lord; and whence is he then his son? And the common people heard him gladly.

神不是死人的　神乃是活人的　神所以你們大錯了。○有一個讀書人來、聽他們辯論、曉得耶穌回答的甚好、就問

他說、衆誡命中、那是第一要緊的呢。耶穌說、衆誡命中第一要緊的就是說、以色列人應當聽、　主我們的　神是獨一無二

的　主、你當盡心盡性盡意盡力愛　主你的　神、這是誡命中第一要緊的、其次也是這樣、就是愛人如己、再沒有比這兩

條誡命更大的了。讀書人對他說好阿、夫子所說的是眞實的、因爲只有一位　神、除了他沒有別的了、若盡心盡性盡意盡

力的愛　主、又愛人如己、就勝過一切燔祭和諸般祭祀。耶穌見他回答有智慧、就說你離　神的國不遠了、以後再沒有人

敢盤問耶穌了。○耶穌在聖殿裏教訓人、就問他們說讀書人爲甚麼說基督是大闢的子孫呢、大闢自己被　聖靈感動說、

主對我　主說坐在我右邊、等我使你的仇敵爲你的腳凳。大闢自己旣稱他爲　主、基督怎麼是大闢的子孫呢。衆人都

歡歡喜喜的聽耶穌講道。

38 ¶ And he said unto them in his doctrine, Beware of the scribes, which love to go in long clothing, and *love* salutations in the marketplaces,

39 And the chief seats in the synagogues, and the uppermost rooms at feasts :

40 Which devour widows' houses, and for a pretence make long prayers: these shall receive greater damnation.

41 ¶ And Jesus sat over against the treasury, and beheld how the people cast money into the treasury : and many that were rich cast in much.

42 And there came a certain poor widow, and she threw in two mites, which make a farthing.

43 And he called *unto him* his disciples, and saith unto them, Verily I say unto you, That this poor widow hath cast more in, than all they which have cast into the treasury :

44 For all *they* did cast in of their abundance ; but she of her want did cast in all that she had, *even* all her living.

CHAPTER XIII.

AND as he went out of the temple, one of his disciples saith unto him, Master, see what manner of stones and what buildings *are here !*

2 And Jesus answering said unto him, Seest thou these great buildings? there shall not be left one stone upon another, that shall not be thrown down.

3 And as he sat upon the mount of Olives, over against the temple, Peter and James and John and Andrew asked him privately,

4 Tell us, when shall these things be ? and what *shall be* the sign when all these things shall be fulfilled ?

5 And Jesus answering them began to say, Take heed lest any *man* deceive you :

○耶穌教訓人的時候又說應當謹防讀書人他們愛穿長衣行走歡喜人在街市上與他請安在會堂裏坐高位、在筵席上坐首座、他們郤侵吞了寡婦的家財、假意作長長的祈禱他們必受更重的刑罰了。○耶穌對銀庫坐著觀看衆人怎樣捐錢入庫有許多財主捐了許多錢有一個貧窮的寡婦來捐兩個小錢就是一個大錢。耶穌就叫門徒來對他們說我實在告訴你們這貧窮的寡婦捐入庫裏的、比衆人捐的還多。因爲衆人是自己有餘、擧出來捐這寡婦是自己不足、反將所有一切養生的擧出來捐。

第十三章

耶穌出了聖殿有一個門徒對他說夫子請看這些石頭這些殿宇是何等的雄壯耶穌對他說、你看見這些大殿宇麼、後來沒有一塊石頭留在石頭上、都必拆毀了。耶穌在橄欖山上、對殿坐著、彼得雅各約翰安得烈、暗暗的問他說請告訴我們甚麼時候有這些事、並且這一切的事、將要臨到的時候、有甚麼預兆呢。耶穌回答說應當謹慎、免得有人迷惑你們。

6 For many shall come in my name, saying, I am *Christ;* and shall deceive many.

7 And when ye shall hear of wars and rumours of wars, be ye not troubled: for *such things* must needs be; but the end *shall* not *be* yet.

8 For nation shall rise against nation, and kingdom against kingdom: and there shall be earthquakes in divers places, and there shall be famines and troubles: these *are* the beginnings of sorrows.

9 But take heed to yourselves: for they shall deliver you up to councils; and in the synagogues ye shall be beaten: and ye shall be brought before rulers and kings for my sake, for a testimony against them.

10 And the gospel must first be published among all nations.

11 But when they shall lead *you,* and deliver you up, take no thought beforehand what ye shall speak, neither do ye premeditate: but whatsoever shall be given you in that hour, that speak ye: for it is not ye that speak, but the Holy Ghost.

12 Now the brother shall betray the brother to death, and the father the son; and children shall rise up against *their* parents, and shall cause them to be put to death.

13 And ye shall be hated of all *men* for my name's sake: but he that shall endure unto the end, the same shall be saved.

14 ¶ But when ye shall see the abomination of desolation, spoken of by Daniel the prophet, standing where it ought not, (let him that readeth understand,) then let them that be in Judea flee to the mountains:

15 And let him that is on the housetop not go down into the house, neither enter *therein,* to take any thing out of his house:

因爲將來有許多人冒我的名來、自稱是基督迷惑許多人。你們聽見打仗和打仗的風聲、不要懼怕、這事是必有的、只是末

日還沒有到。民要攻打民、國要攻打國、地震、饑荒、反亂、各處都有、這是災難的起頭。你們應當自己謹愼、人爲我要將你們解

到公會、在會堂裏鞭打、又叫你們站在君王侯伯面前作見證、然而福音必先傳遍萬國。人將你們送官的時候、不要先籌算

怎麼說話、也不要思慮、到那時候、賜給你們甚麼話、你們就說甚麼話、因爲不是你們自己說的、乃是 聖靈說的。那時弟兄

要將弟兄、父親要將兒子、送到死地、兒女要與父母爲仇、害死他們。你們必要爲我的名、被衆人怨恨、惟有忍耐到底的、必定

得救。你們看見先知但以理所說殘暴可憎的物、站在不當站的地方、讀這經的人、應當思想、那時候、住在猶太的人、應當逃

到山上、在房上的、不要下來進屋子、也不要進去取東西、

16 And let him that is in the field not turn back again for to take up his garment.

17 But woe to them that are with child, and to them that give suck in those days !

18 And pray ye that your flight be not in the winter.

19 For *in* those days shall be affliction, such as was not from the beginning of the creation which God created unto this time, neither shall be.

20 And except that the Lord had shortened those days, no flesh should be saved : but for the elect's sake, whom he hath chosen, he hath shortened the days.

21 And then if any man shall say to you, Lo, here *is* Christ; or, lo, *he is* there ; believe *him* not :

22 For false Christs and false prophets shall rise, and shall shew signs and wonders, to seduce, if *it were* possible, even the elect.

23 But take ye heed : behold, I have foretold you all things.

24 ¶ But in those days, after that tribulation, the sun shall be darkened, and the moon shall not give her light,

25 And the stars of heaven shall fall, and the powers that are in heaven shall be shaken.

26 And then shall they see the Son of man coming in the clouds with great power and glory.

27 And then shall he send his angels, and shall gather together his elect from the four winds, from the uttermost part of the earth to the uttermost part of heaven.

28 Now learn a parable of the fig tree : When her branch is yet tender, and putteth forth leaves, ye know that summer is near :

29 So ye in like manner, when ye shall see these things come to pass, know that it is nigh, *even* at the doors.

在田裏的、不要回家取衣服那時候懷孕的和乳養嬰孩的婦人有禍了你們應當祈禱免得你們在冬天逃走。因爲那時必

有災難從　神創造萬物直到如今沒有這樣的災難後來也必沒有。

主若不滅少那日子就沒有一個人得救只是爲那蒙揀選的人已經將那日子滅少了。那時若有人告訴你們說基督在這裏基督在那裏你們不可信因爲假基督假先知將

要起來、施行異蹟奇事若能迷惑揀選的人也就迷惑了你們須要謹愼這事我都預先告訴你們。在那些日子、那災難以

後日頭必要黑暗月不放光衆星從天上墜落天象都要震動那時衆人要看見人子有大權柄大榮耀駕著雲來那時必差

遣他的使者、從四方從地極直到天邊將所揀選的人、都招聚了來。你們可以拏無花果樹作比方當樹枝柔嫩發葉的時候、

就曉得夏天快到了這樣、你們看見這些兆頭也就曉得時候近了已在門前了。

30 Verily I say unto you, that this generation shall not pass, till all these things be done.

31 Heaven and earth shall pass away: but my words shall not pass away.

32 ¶ But of that day and *that* hour knoweth no man, no, not the angels which are in heaven, neither the Son, but the Father.

33 Take ye heed, watch and pray: for ye know not when the time is.

34 *For the Son of man is* as a man taking a far journey, who left his house, and gave authority to his servants, and to every man his work, and commanded the porter to watch.

35 Watch ye therefore: for ye know not when the master of the house cometh, at even, or at midnight, or at the cockcrowing, or in the morning:

36 Lest coming suddenly he find you sleeping.

37 And what I say unto you I say unto all, Watch.

CHAPTER XIV.

AFTER two days was *the feast of* the passover, and of unleavened bread: and the chief priests and the scribes sought how they might take him by craft, and put *him* to death.

2 But they said, Not on the feast *day*, lest there be an uproar of the people.

3 ¶ And being in Bethany, in the house of Simon the leper, as he sat at meat, there came a woman having an alabaster box of ointment of spikenard very precious; and she brake the box, and poured *it* on his head.

4 And there were some that had indignation within themselves, and said, Why was this waste of the ointment made?

5 For it might have been sold for more than three hundred pence, and have been given to the poor. And they murmured against her.

我實在告訴你們、這一代還沒有過去這些事都必成就。天地必廢、我的話斷不能廢、只是那日子、那時候、沒有人知道、就是在天上的使者也不知道子也不知道只有　父知道。○你們應當謹慎儆醒祈禱、因爲你們不曉得這日期幾時來到。人子如同一個人離家往遠處去將權柄交給僕人分派各人當做的事又吩咐看門的儆醒。所以你們應當儆醒、因爲你們不曉得家主甚麼時候回來、或晚上、或雞叫、或早晨、恐怕他忽然回來、看見你們睡著了。我所告訴你們的、我也告訴衆人、

應當儆醒。

第十四章

過了兩日是逾越節又叫除酵節、衆祭司長和讀書人商議要用詭計捉拏耶穌殺他只是說當節的日子、不可拏他恐怕百姓生亂。○耶穌在伯大尼長過癩的西門家裏坐席、有一個婦人拏著玉盒裏面盛著至眞至貴的那達香膏前來、揭開玉盒、將膏澆在耶穌的頭上、有幾個人心中不歡喜說爲甚麼這樣糜費香膏呢、這香膏可以賣三十多兩銀子、賙濟窮人他們就怨恨那婦人。

6 And Jesus said, Let her alone;
why trouble ye her? she hath wrought
a good work on me.

7 For ye have the poor with you
always, and whensoever ye will ye
may do them good: but me ye have
not always.

8 She hath done what she could:
she is come aforehand to anoint my
body to the burying.

9 Verily I say unto you, Wheresoever this gospel shall be preached
throughout the whole world, *this* also
that she hath done shall be spoken of
for a memorial of her.

10 ¶ And Judas Iscariot, one of
the twelve, went unto the chief priests,
to betray him unto them.

11 And when they heard *it*, they
were glad, and promised to give him
money. And he sought how he might
conveniently betray him.

12 ¶ And the first day of unleavened bread, when they killed the
passover, his disciples said unto him,
Where wilt thou that we go and
prepare that thou mayest eat the
passover?

13 And he sendeth forth two of his
disciples, and saith unto them, Go ye
into the city, and there shall meet
you a man bearing a pitcher of water:
follow him.

14 And wheresoever he shall go in,
say ye to the goodman of the house,
The Master saith, Where is the guestchamber, where I shall eat the passover with my disciples?

15 And he will shew you a large
upper room furnished *and* prepared:
there make ready for us.

16 And his disciples went forth,
and came into the city, and found as
he had said unto them: and they
made ready the passover.

17 And in the evening he cometh
with the twelve.

耶穌說你們由他罷爲甚麼難爲他呢他向我所作的是好事窮人常和你們在一處你們善待窮人臨時都可以只是我不常和你們在一處這婦人所作的是盡他的力量他將香膏澆在我身上是豫備我安葬的事我實在告訴你們普天之下無論在何處傳福音必要述說這婦人所行的叫人記念他十二門徒裏有一個以色加畧猶大去見祭司長要將耶穌賣給他們他們聽見就歡喜了應許給他銀子猶大就尋找機會要賣耶穌○除酵節的頭一日宰逾越節羔羊的時候門徒對耶穌說你喫逾越節的羔羊要我們往那裏去豫備耶穌差遣兩個門徒吩咐他們說你們進城去必遇見一個拏水瓶的人就跟著他他進那一家去你們就對那一家的主人說夫子說客房在那裏我和門徒要在裏面喫逾越節的筵席他必指給你們一間大樓擺設齊整就在那裏爲我們豫備門徒出去進了城所遇見的果然與耶穌對他們所說的一樣他們就豫備了逾越節的筵席○到了晚上耶穌和十二門徒來坐席

18 And as they sat and did eat, Jesus said, Verily I say unto you, One of you which eateth with me shall betray me.

19 And they began to be sorrowful, and to say unto him one by one, *Is it I?* and another *said, Is* it I?

20 And he answered and said unto them, *It is* one of the twelve, that dippeth with me in the dish.

21 The Son of man indeed goeth, as it is written of him: but woe to that man by whom the Son of man is betrayed! good were it for that man if he had never been born.

22 ¶ And as they did eat, Jesus took bread, and blessed, and brake *it,* and gave to them, and said, Take, eat; this is my body.

23 And he took the cup, and when he had given thanks, he gave *it* to them: and they all drank of it.

24 And he said unto them, This is my blood of the new testament, which is shed for many.

25 Verily I say unto you, I will drink no more of the fruit of the vine, until that day that I drink it new in the kingdom of God.

26 ¶ And when they had sung a hymn, they went out into the mount of Olives.

27 And Jesus saith unto them, All ye shall be offended because of me this night: for it is written, I will smite the Shepherd, and the sheep shall be scattered.

28 But after that I am risen, I will go before you into Galilee.

29 But Peter said unto him, Although all shall be offended, yet *will* not I.

30 And Jesus saith unto him, Verily I say unto thee, That this day, *even* in this night, before the cock crow twice, thou shalt deny me thrice.

正喫的時候、耶穌說我實在告訴你們、你們中間有一個和我同吃的人、要賣我了門徒憂愁起來、一個一個的問耶穌說是

我麼、是我麼。耶穌囘答說十二個人裏有一個和我蘸乎在盤子裏的、就是他人子必要照著經上所指著他說的話去世只

是賣人子的人必定有禍這人倒不如不生在世上吃的時候、耶穌擘起餅來、祝謝了、擘開分給門徒、說你們擘這個吃這是

我的身體又擧起盃來、祝謝了、遞給門徒他們都喝了耶穌對他們說、這是我的血就是新約的血爲衆人流出來的我實在

告訴你們、從今日直到我和你們在　神國裏喝新酒那日子、我不再喝這葡萄汁了。○他們歌了詩就出來、往橄欖山去耶

穌對他們說這夜裏你們都要厭棄我因爲經上說我將打牧羊的、羣羊就都散了。我復活之後、要在你們以先往加利利去。

彼得說、衆人雖然厭棄你、我必不厭棄你。耶穌說我實在告訴你這夜裏雞叫第二次以先、你要三次說不認識我。

31 But he spake the more vehemently, If I should die with thee, I will not deny thee in any wise. Likewise also said they all.

32 And they came to a place which was named Gethsemane: and he saith to his disciples, Sit ye here, while I shall pray.

33 And he taketh with him Peter and James and John, and began to be sore amazed, and to be very heavy;

34 And saith unto them, My soul is exceeding sorrowful unto death: tarry ye here, and watch.

35 And he went forward a little, and fell on the ground, and prayed that, if it were possible, the hour might pass from him.

36 And he said, Abba, Father, all things *are* possible unto thee; take away this cup from me: nevertheless, not what I will, but what thou wilt.

37 And he cometh, and findeth them sleeping, and saith unto Peter, Simon, sleepest thou? couldest not thou watch one hour?

38 Watch ye and pray, lest ye enter into temptation. The spirit truly *is* ready, but the flesh *is* weak.

39 And again he went away, and prayed, and spake the same words.

40 And when he returned, he found them asleep again, (for their eyes were heavy,) neither wist they what to answer him.

41 And he cometh the third time, and saith unto them, Sleep on now, and take *your* rest: it is enough, the hour is come; behold, the Son of man is betrayed into the hands of sinners.

42 Rise up, let us go; lo, he that betrayeth me is at hand.

43 ¶ And immediately, while he yet spake, cometh Judas, one of the twelve, and with him a great multitude with swords and staves, from the chief priests and the scribes and the elders.

彼得極力的說、我就是和你同死、決不說不認識你。衆門徒也都這樣說他們、到了一個地方、名叫客西馬尼耶穌對門徒說、

你們坐在這裏等我去禱告、於是帶了彼得雅各約翰同去、就驚恐悲傷、對他們說、我心裏甚是憂傷、幾乎要死、你們在這裏

等候儆醒。他就往前行了幾步俯伏在地、祈禱說、假若可行、就叫這時候過去、又說、

一盃離開我、但不要從我的意思、要從你的意思、耶穌回來、看見門徒睡覺、對彼得說、西門、你睡覺麼、不能儆醒片時麼。應當

儆醒祈禱免得入了迷惑、心裏固然願意身子卻輭弱了。耶穌又去禱告和先前一樣說、

眼時困倦了他們也不知道怎樣回答耶穌。第三次來對他們說、現在你們仍然睡覺安息罷了、時候到了、人子被賣到惡人

手裏了、起來、我們去罷、賣我的人離這裏不遠了。〇說話之間、十二門徒裏的猶大帶著許多人手擎刀棒、從祭司長讀書人

阿巴父呵、你是無所不能的、求你叫這

和長老那裏來。

44 And he that betrayed him had given them a token, saying, Whomsoever I shall kiss, that same is he; take him, and lead *him* away safely.

45 And as soon as he was come, he goeth straightway to him, and saith, Master, Master; and kissed him.

46 ¶ And they laid their hands on him, and took him.

47 And one of them that stood by drew a sword, and smote a servant of the high priest, and cut off his ear.

48 And Jesus answered and said unto them, Are ye come out, as against a thief, with swords and *with* staves to take me?

49 I was daily with you in the temple teaching, and ye took me not: but the Scriptures must be fulfilled.

50 And they all forsook him and fled.

51 And there followed him a certain young man, having a linen cloth cast about *his* naked *body*; and the young men laid hold on him:

52 And he left the linen cloth, and fled from them naked.

53 ¶ And they led Jesus away to the high priest: and with him were assembled all the chief priests and the elders and the scribes.

54 And Peter followed him afar off, even into the palace of the high priest: and he sat with the servants, and warmed himself at the fire.

55 And the chief priests and all the council sought for witness against Jesus to put him to death; and found none.

56 For many bare false witness against him, but their witness agreed not together.

57 And there arose certain, and bare false witness against him, saying,

58 We heard him say, I will destroy this temple that is made with hands, and within three days I will build another made without hands.

賣耶穌的人、曾與他們定一個暗號說、我與誰親嘴誰就是那人、你們將他捉住小心帶去。

就來到耶穌面前說夫子、夫子、便和他親嘴、那些人就下手捉住耶穌。

旁邊站著的有一個人拔出刀來、砍祭司長的僕人、削掉了他一個耳朵。

耶穌對衆人說、你們帶著刀棒來捉我、如同捉賊麼、我日日坐在聖殿裏敎訓人、和你們在一處、你們反倒不拏我、但這事成了、爲要應驗經上的話。

門徒都離開耶穌逃走了。○衆人將耶穌解到大祭司面前衆祭司長長老和讀書人都在那裏聚會彼得遠遠的跟隨耶穌進入大祭司的院、

和差役同坐烤火衆祭司長和全公會的人尋找見證、控告耶穌要治死他、卻尋不著、因爲有許多人作假見證來控告他、只

是他們所見證的不合、又有幾個人起來作假見證告他說我們聽見這個人說、我要拆毀這人手所建造的殿、三日內另建

有一個少年人身上只披著蔴布、跟隨耶穌、有幾個兵將他捉住他就丟了蔴布、赤著身子逃走了。

造一座殿、那殿不是人手所建造的。

59 But neither so did their witness agree together.

60 And the high priest stood up in the midst, and asked Jesus, saying, Answerest thou nothing? what *is it which* these witness against thee?

61 But he held his peace, and answered nothing. Again the high priest asked him, and said unto him, Art thou the Christ, the Son of the Blessed?

62 And Jesus said, I am: and ye shall see the Son of man sitting on the right hand of power, and coming in the clouds of heaven.

63 Then the high priest rent his clothes, and saith, What need we any further witnesses?

64 Ye have heard the blasphemy: what think ye? And they all condemned him to be guilty of death.

65 And some began to spit on him, and to cover his face, and to buffet him, and to say unto him, Prophesy: and the servants did strike him with the palms of their hands.

66 ¶ And as Peter was beneath in the palace, there cometh one of the maids of the high priest:

67 And when she saw Peter warming himself, she looked upon him, and said, And thou also wast with Jesus of Nazareth.

68 But he denied, saying, I know not, neither understand I what thou sayest. And he went out into the porch; and the cock crew.

69 And a maid saw him again, and began to say to them that stood by, This is *one* of them.

70 And he denied it again. And a little after, they that stood by said again to Peter, Surely thou art *one* of them: for thou art a Galilean, and thy speech agreeth *thereto*.

71 But he began to curse and to swear, *saying*, I know not this man of whom ye speak.

但他們的見證、也是不合。大祭司起來站在中間、問耶穌說、你沒有話對答麼這些人作見證告你的是甚麼、耶穌閉口、一句不答、大祭司又問他說你是當稱頌的　神的兒子基督不是、耶穌說、我是的、後來你們要看見人子、坐在有大權的　主的右邊、駕著天上的雲降臨、大祭司就斯開衣服說、我們何必尋別的見證呢、你們巳經聽見他僭妄的話了、你們的意思如何。衆人就將他定成死罪、有人吐唾沫在他身上、又遮住他的臉、用拳頭打他、對他說你是先知、可說打你的是誰、衆僕人也用手掌打他、彼得在外院子裏大祭司的一個使女出來、見了彼得烤火、就看著他、說你也是跟從拏撒勒人耶穌的罷、彼得不認說、我不知道、也不明白你說的是甚麼、於是出來、到了門前、雞就叫了、又有一個使女看見他、對旁邊站著的人說、這也是他們一黨的人、彼得又不認、過了不多的時候、旁邊站著的人、又對彼得說、你眞是他們一黨的、因爲你是加利利的人、你的口音也像彼得發咒起督的說你們所說的這個人、我不認識。

72 And the second time the cock crew. And Peter called to mind the word that Jesus said unto him, Before the cock crow twice, thou shalt deny me thrice. And when he thought thereon, he wept.

CHAPTER XV.

AND straightway in the morning the chief priests held a consultation with the elders and scribes and the whole council, and bound Jesus, and carried *him* away, and delivered *him* to Pilate.

2 And Pilate asked him, Art thou the King of the Jews? And he answering said unto him, Thou sayest *it*.

3 And the chief priests accused him of many things; but he answered nothing.

4 And Pilate asked him again, saying, Answerest thou nothing? behold how many things they witness against thee.

5 But Jesus yet answered nothing; so that Pilate marvelled.

6 Now at *that* feast he released unto them one prisoner, whomsoever they desired.

7 And there was *one* named Barabbas, *which lay* bound with them that had made insurrection with him, who had committed murder in the insurrection.

8 And the multitude crying aloud began to desire *him to do* as he had ever done unto them.

9 But Pilate answered them, saying, Will ye that I release unto you the King of the Jews?

10 For he knew that the chief priests had delivered him for envy.

11 But the chief priests moved the people, that he should rather release Barabbas unto them.

12 And Pilate answered and said again unto them, What will ye then that I shall do *unto him* whom ye call the King of the Jews?

雞就叫了第二次、於是彼得想起耶穌所說雞叫第二次之先、你要三次說不認識我的話、再三思念就哭了。

第十五章

一到了清早衆祭司長長老讀書人和全公會的人、大家商議、就將耶穌綁上、解交彼拉多、二彼拉多問他說、你是猶太人的王麼、耶穌回答說、你說的是、三衆祭司長將許多的事告他、彼拉多又問他說、他們作見證告你這許多的事、你不回答麼、耶穌仍不同答、彼拉多以爲希奇、五每到這節、方伯照百姓所求的、給他們釋放一個囚犯、有一個人名叫巴拉巴、和造反的人一同捆綁、因造反的時候、曾殺過人、八衆人大聲求方伯照常例辦理、彼拉多同答說、你們要我釋放猶太人的王麼、彼拉多說這話、因爲知道衆祭司長將耶穌解了來、是因爲娼妬耶穌、祭司長挑唆衆人、求釋放巴拉巴、彼拉多又說、你們所稱爲猶太人的王的、要我怎樣辦呢。

13 And they cried out again, Crucify him.

14 Then Pilate said unto them, Why, what evil hath he done ? And they cried out the more exceedingly, Crucify him.

15 ¶ And *so* Pilate, willing to content the people, released Barabbas unto them, and delivered Jesus, when he had scourged *him*, to be crucified.

16 And the soldiers led him away into the hall, called Pretorium ; and they call together the whole band.

17 And they clothed him with purple, and platted a crown of thorns, and put it about his *head,*

18 And began to salute him, Hail, King of the Jews !

19 And they smote him on the head with a reed, and did spit upon him, and bowing *their* knees worshipped him.

20 And when they had mocked him, they took off the purple from him, and put his own clothes on him, and led him out to crucify him.

21 And they compel one Simon a Cyrenian, who passed by, coming out of the country, the father of Alexander and Rufus, to bear his cross.

22 And they bring him unto the place Golgotha, which is, being interpreted, The place of a skull.

23 And they gave him to drink wine mingled with myrrh : but he received *it* not.

24 And when they had crucified him, they parted his garments, casting lots upon them, what every man should take.

25 And it was the third hour, and they crucified him.

26 And the superscription of his accusation was written over, THE KING OF THE JEWS.

27 And with him they crucify two thieves ; the one on his right hand, and the other on his left.

衆人又喊叫說釘他在十字架上、彼拉多說、他作了甚麼惡事、衆人越發喊叫說、釘他在十字架上、彼拉多要作百姓所歡喜

的事、就放了巴拉巴、將耶穌鞭打了、交給人釘在十字架上、兵丁領耶穌進了院內、就是公堂、聚齊了全營的兵、擊著紫袍給

他穿上、又用枳棘編作冕、給他戴上、就給他請安、說、請猶太人的王安、又拏一根葦子打他的頭、吐唾沫在他身上跪下拜他。

戲弄完了、脫了紫袍給他穿上原舊的衣服、拉他出來、要釘在十字架上、有一個古利奈人、名叫西門、就是亞力山大和魯孚

的父親、從鄉下來、經過那地方、衆人勉强他背著耶穌的十字架、他們帶耶穌到了一個地方、名叫各各他、繙出來就是髑髏

處、將沒藥調和的酒給耶穌喝、耶穌不肯喝。他們將他釘在十字架上、拈鬮分他的衣服、看是誰得甚麼、各釘他在十字架上、是

巳初時分。在上面寫著告他的話說、猶太人的王。他們又將兩個强盜和他同釘十字架、一個在左邊、一個在右邊、

28 And the Scripture was fulfilled, which saith, And he was numbered with the transgressors.

29 And they that passed by railed on him, wagging their heads, and saying, Ah, thou that destroyest the temple, and buildest it in three days,

30 Save thyself, and come down from the cross.

31 Likewise also the chief priests mocking said among themselves with the scribes, He saved others; himself he cannot save.

32 Let Christ the king of Israel descend now from the cross, that we may see and believe. And they that were crucified with him reviled him.

33 And when the sixth hour was come, there was darkness over the whole land until the ninth hour.

34 And at the ninth hour Jesus cried with a loud voice, saying, Eloi, Eloi, lama sabachthani? which is, being interpreted, My God, my God, why hast thou forsaken me?

35 And some of them that stood by, when they heard it, said, Behold, he calleth Elias.

36 And one ran and filled a sponge full of vinegar, and put it on a reed, and gave him to drink, saying, Let alone; let us see whether Elias will come to take him down.

37 And Jesus cried with a loud voice, and gave up the ghost.

38 And the vail of the temple was rent in twain from the top to the bottom.

39 ¶ And when the centurion, which stood over against him, saw that he so cried out, and gave up the ghost, he said, Truly this man was the Son of God.

40 There were also women looking on afar off: among whom was Mary Magdalene, and Mary the mother of James the less and of Joses, and Salome;

這就應了經上的話說人將他列在罪犯中從那裏經過的人譏誚耶穌搖著頭說你這拆毀聖殿、三日又建造起來的、現在

可以救自己從十字架上下來罷祭司長和讀書人大家也是這樣戲弄他、說他救別人、倒不能救自己以色列的王基督、

如今可以從十字架上下來、我們看見就信了、和他同釘的人也罵他。從午正到申初、遍地都黑暗了。申初時候耶穌大聲喊

叫說以羅伊以羅拉馬撒巴各大尼、繙出來、就是我　神我　神爲甚麼離了我。旁邊站著的有幾個人聽見就說他呼叫

以利亞。有一個人跑來將海絨浸在醋裏綁在葦子上、送給他喝、說且等著看以利亞來取他下來、不來取他下來。耶穌大聲

喊叫氣就斷了。殿裏的幔子從上到下、裂爲兩半對面站著的百夫長看見耶穌這樣喊叫斷氣就說這人眞是　神的兒子

了。○有幾個婦人遠遠的觀看內中有抹大拉的馬利亞和小雅各並約西的母親馬利亞又有撒羅米。

41 Who also, when he was in Galilee, followed him, and ministered unto him; and many other women which came up with him unto Jerusalem.

42 ¶ And now when the even was come, because it was the preparation, that is, the day before the sabbath,

43 Joseph of Arimathea, an honourable counsellor, which also waited for the kingdom of God, came, and went in boldly unto Pilate, and craved the body of Jesus.

44 And Pilate marvelled if he were already dead: and calling *unto him* the centurion, he asked him whether he had been any while dead.

45 And when he knew *it* of the centurion, he gave the body to Joseph.

46 And he bought fine linen, and took him down, and wrapped him in the linen, and laid him in a sepulchre which was hewn out of a rock, and rolled a stone unto the door of the sepulchre.

47 And Mary Magdalene and Mary *the mother* of Joses beheld where he was laid.

CHAPTER XVI.

AND when the sabbath was past, Mary Magdalene, and Mary the *mother* of James, and Salome, had bought sweet spices, that they might come and anoint him.

2 And very early in the morning, the first *day* of the week, they came unto the sepulchre at the rising of the sun.

3 And they said among themselves, Who shall roll us away the stone from the door of the sepulchre?

4 And when they looked, they saw that the stone was rolled away: for it was very great.

5 And entering into the sepulchre, they saw a young man sitting on the right side, clothed in a long white garment; and they were affrighted.

這些婦人、就是耶穌在加利利的時候、跟隨服事耶穌的、還有和耶穌同上耶路撒冷的許多婦人在那裏觀看○這日是豫備安息日的日子、就是安息日的前一日時候已經晚了。有亞力馬太的人約瑟前來、他是尊貴的議士、也是盼望　神國的、放膽進去見彼拉多求耶穌的身體。彼拉多詫異耶穌已經死了、就叫百夫長來、問他死的久不久、既從百夫長的話得知實情、就將耶穌的身體賜給約瑟約瑟買了細蔴布、將耶穌的身體取下來、用細蔴布裹好、安葬在墳墓裏這墳墓是鑿在磐石裏的、又將一塊石頭轉到墓門口抹大拉的馬利亞和約西的母親馬利亞都看見他安葬的地方

第十六章

安息日過了、抹大拉的馬利亞、和雅各的母親馬利亞、並撒羅米、買了香料要去抹耶穌的身體七日的頭一日、清早、日出的時候、他們來到墳墓前、大家說誰爲我們將墓門口的石頭轉開呢。原來那石頭甚大他們一望、就看見已經轉開了、進了墳就見一個少年人坐在右邊、穿著白袍、那些婦人驚駭起來。

6 And he saith unto them, Be not affrighted: ye seek Jesus of Nazareth, which was crucified: he is risen; he is not here: behold the place where they laid him.

7 But go your way, tell his disciples and Peter that he goeth before you into Galilee: there shall ye see him, as he said unto you.

8 And they went out quickly, and fled from the sepulchre; for they trembled and were amazed: neither said they any thing to any *man*; for they were afraid.

9 ¶ Now when *Jesus* was risen early the first *day* of the week, he appeared first to Mary Magdalene, out of whom he had cast seven devils.

10 *And* she went and told them that had been with him, as they mourned and wept.

11 And they, when they had heard that he was alive, and had been seen of her, believed not.

12 ¶ After that he appeared in another form unto two of them, as they walked, and went into the country.

13 And they went and told *it* unto the residue: neither believed they them.

14 ¶ Afterward he appeared unto the eleven as they sat at meat, and upbraided them with their unbelief and hardness of heart, because they believed not them which had seen him after he was risen.

15 And he said unto them, Go ye into all the world, and preach the gospel to every creature.

16 He that believeth and is baptized shall be saved; but he that believeth not shall be damned.

17 And these signs shall follow them that believe; In my name shall they cast out devils; they shall speak with new tongues;

少年人對他們說、不要驚駭、你們尋找釘十字架的拏撒勒人耶穌、他已經復活、不在這裏了、你們來看安葬他的地方、你們

且去告訴他的門徒、和彼得說、耶穌比你們先到加利利去了、在那裏可以見他、正如他從前告訴你們的話、那些婦人急忙

出來、從墳墓前跑回去、又戰兢又驚駭、一句話也不告訴人、因爲他們甚懼怕○耶穌在七日的頭一日清早復活、先顯現給

抹大拉的馬利亞看見、耶穌曾從這馬利亞身上逐出七個鬼、這婦人去告訴那向來跟隨耶穌的人、那時他們正哭泣悲哀、他

們聽見耶穌復活、被這婦人看見、郤不肯信、後來他們中間有兩個人往鄉下去、走路的時候、耶穌改變相貌、顯現給他們看、

這兩個人就去告訴其餘的門徒、還是不信、後來十一個門徒坐席的時候、耶穌顯現給他們看、責備他們心裏

剛硬不信、因爲他復活以後、有人看見他、告訴他們、他們仍是不信、耶穌對他們說、你們往普天下去、傳福音與萬民聽信而

受洗的、必要得救、不信的、必要定他的罪、信的人必能施行奇事、靠我的名趕鬼、說各國的方言、

18 They shall take up serpents; and if they drink any deadly thing, it shall not hurt them; they shall lay hands on the sick, and they shall recover.

19 ¶ So then, after the Lord had spoken unto them, he was received up into heaven, and sat on the right hand of God.

20 And they went forth, and preached every where, the Lord working with *them*, and confirming the word with signs following. Amen.

見證所傳的道阿們。

福音、主也輔助他們施行奇事、

神的右邊門徒出去往各處宣講

他們說完了話就升了天坐在

手按病人病人就好了。○ 主和

手能拏蛇若喝了毒物也不受害

Lightning Source UK Ltd.
Milton Keynes UK
UKOW021946090512

192265UK00005B/15/P